This is the most comprehensive exploration of this important subject that I have read. Thorough and thoughtful, it is an essential text for students of God's Word, Bible teachers, and pastors. With gratitude to the author, I recommend this book to all.

—JOHN DAWSON
PRESIDENT EMERITUS/GLOBAL CONVENER,
YOUTH WITH A MISSION INTERNATIONAL

Our own blood courses through our veins and removes impurities from our bodies, a process without which we die. But it also brings life-giving nutrients, without which we also die. Blood is in the cross and the resurrection. Ray Beeson takes us beyond common metaphorical terminology and explores the rich meaning that life is indeed in the blood.

—DR. NEIL T. ANDERSON
FOUNDER AND PRESIDENT EMERITUS,
FREEDOM IN CHRIST MINISTRIES

This is a truly significant and comprehensive study of the blood of Jesus Christ, detailing the importance of the blood covenant and the inherent power of the blood that is to be manifested in the lives of believers. Drink deeply as you read its pages, for—as the disciples of Jesus—you hold in your hands the sacred cup, "the new testament in my blood, which is shed for you" (Luke 22:20, KJV).

—PATRICIA HULSEY
VICE PRESIDENT, HARVESTIME INTERNATIONAL NETWORK

It is with great joy I endorse this powerful book by Ray Beeson. Satan hates the blood of Jesus, the cross of Jesus, and the resurrection of Jesus. Anything that expounds and illuminates the blood of Jesus is sure to bring deliverance and healing. Let your spirit saturate in the powerful principles of the blood of Jesus. Your miracle could be present by the end of this book!

—LARRY STOCKSTILL
TEACHING PASTOR, BETHANY WORLD OUTREACH CHURCH
AUTHOR, THE REMNANT

Ray Beeson has effectively taken the unique and life-altering core principle of the Bible—God's blood covenant with humanity—and, I feel, faithfully overviewed and explained its relationships throughout Scripture.

Beeson's message intends to show that the entire Bible fits into a covenant framework rather than, as he says, the idea that its covenants served only for a particular reason within a certain time period. He has done an excellent job in making that case and in examining the ways God unites humanity to Himself through covenants.

Beeson says blood is so significant in Scripture that it cannot be overlooked and that God has always used blood as the ink in His agreements (or covenants) with mankind. This book is thorough and comprehensive, and it gives readers a compelling view of God's wondrous, redemptive, and transformational intervention into mankind's sin-burdened life through His blood covenant.

—T. Ray Rachels
Member, Assemblies of God General Council
Executive Presbytery

This is an in-depth study of the power of the blood of Christ that points the reader to a biblical understanding of the blood. This book will strengthen your faith and inspire your prayers. It will establish you in a firm place of knowing the power in the name of Jesus.

—Frank Damazio
Lead pastor, City Bible Church
Chairman, Ministers Fellowship International

I cannot recall reading a book on the subject of Christ's blood that included so many valuable insights. Ray Beeson has managed to give us what I believe will be a classic. I intend to keep this book very close at hand. It contains so many elements that are practical for a disciple of Jesus. For so many years there has been great misunderstanding about the blood. Like so many truths of the Word, you will find extremes—from those who would see the blood as a "magic wand" to those who see it only in a historical context. The truth is that there is great power in the blood. What we need is a skilled writer and student of the Word to convey its wondrous truths. Ray Beeson is that skilled writer. He invites us to a journey, a journey that will cause us to worship our God for His unspeakable love and provision. That love and those provisions are *signed in blood.*

—CHRIS HAYWARD
PRESIDENT, CLEANSING STREAM MINISTRIES

This book expounds on the greatest truth of the Bible, for without the shedding of blood there is *no* remission of sin. It will inspire you to see the importance of this wonderful biblical truth that is found in both the Old and New Testaments. Ray brings out these truths in a very vivid way that will give you a new appreciation for the blood of Jesus and the work of the cross.

—DICK IVERSON
FOUNDER, MINISTERS FELLOWSHIP INTERNATIONAL

This book causes the reader to renew their covenant commitment to God. Whenever God relates to anyone, He enters into a binding, loving, and eternal relationship with the individual He is relating to. A covenant is a bond that creates a relationship that is intimate, durable, and not based on personal feelings. In this book Ray takes the reader from *consumer* to *covenant relationship*! You will meet the God of covenant as you read this life-changing book.

—JUDE FOUQUIER
PASTOR, THE CITY CHURCH VENTURA (CALIFORNIA)

SIGNED IN HIS BLOOD

RAY BEESON

CHARISMA
HOUSE

Most CHARISMA HOUSE BOOK GROUP products are available at special quantity discounts for bulk purchase for sales promotions, premiums, fund-raising, and educational needs. For details, write Charisma House Book Group, 600 Rinehart Road, Lake Mary, Florida 32746, or telephone (407) 333-0600.

SIGNED IN HIS BLOOD by Ray Beeson
Published by Charisma House
Charisma Media/Charisma House Book Group
600 Rinehart Road
Lake Mary, Florida 32746
www.charismahouse.com

Unless otherwise noted, all Scripture quotations are from the New King James Version of the Bible. Copyright © 1979, 1980, 1982 by Thomas Nelson, Inc., publishers. Used by permission.

Scripture quotations marked ESV are from the Holy Bible, English Standard Version. Copyright © 2001 by Crossway Bibles, a division of Good News Publishers. Used by permission.

Scripture quotations marked KJV are from the King James Version of the Bible.

Scripture quotations marked NCV are from The Holy Bible, New Century Version. Copyright © 1987, 1988, 1991 by Word Publishing, Dallas, Texas 75039. Used by permission.

Scripture quotations marked NIV are from the Holy Bible, New International Version. Copyright © 1973, 1978, 1984, International Bible Society. Used by permission.

Cover design by Lisa Rae Cox
Design Director: Bill Johnson

Visit the author's website at www.overcomersministries.net.

Library of Congress Cataloging-in-Publication Data:
An application to register this book for cataloging has been submitted to the Library of Congress.
International Standard Book Number: 978-1-62136-274-6
E-book ISBN: 978-1-62136-275-3

While the author has made every effort to provide accurate telephone numbers and Internet addresses at the time of publication, neither the publisher nor the author assumes any responsibility for errors or for changes that occur after publication.

First edition

14 15 16 17 18 — 987654321
Printed in the United States of America

To Linda:
My wife,
Companion,
Friend.

Contents

Acknowledgments

So many good things happen only when someone comes alongside you and adds his own expertise to your efforts. Four men have done just that for me.

Pastor Jack Hayford knew I had been writing this book for many years. When I told him I had no plans to publish it, he felt it would be valuable to the body of Christ and helped in moving it forward to publication.

Rick Kline is no doubt the most read man I have ever met. He wades through books with remarkable focus. His insights and help have been most valuable.

Darrel Faxon is not only a wonderful friend but also a man who knows God's Word and shares it abundantly. He has one of the most profound understandings of the gospel of almost any person I have met, and his insights into this topic have been profound.

Jim Ayars took the time to read through the manuscript with me personally. His deep knowledge of both Greek and Hebrew and his love for the Scriptures have brought fresh insights to my own thinking.

Thanks to all of you for helping to make this book a reality.

Foreword

Ray Beeson's writings have been a source of solid teaching, biblical soundness, and practical application for years. There were occasions in my pastorate at The Church On The Way in Van Nuys, California, that his works were utilized for group studies. On one occasion I led the congregation through his book *Strategic Spiritual Warfare* as part of our congregation-wide Summer Studies Together, which involved thousands who participated in eight midweek gatherings. So I'm sure it's clear—I believe in this author as someone who provides the church *anywhere* with fresh insight, biblical revelation, and life-touching, soul-stretching, spirit-enriching material. *Signed in His Blood* is but one more of Ray's books that verify that claim.

Having heard a CD recording of a sermon he preached that had been drawn from the content you have in hand, I asked him, "Is that in book form?" He said that a small part of it had been used in a few locations. I indicated my feeling of concern: "Brother, that is a very unsatisfying answer!" I felt constrained of God's Spirit to strongly urge him to approach a publisher. In fact, to expedite and assure action, I offered to make a call and set up the contact for my friend!

I relate that to you in introducing *Signed in His Blood* because of my convictions about the truth it focuses and the transforming power and ministry it will beget in each earnest, wisdom-seeking reader. I am not fearful of overstating the value, enrichment, and practical tools you'll find here—tools for ministering to others, tools for spiritual warfare, and truths that, if shared, will move people you love or serve or teach toward pathways of dynamic service and applied wisdom. (By the way, this book is just plain interesting at points as well!) It is laced with unforgettable takeaways for your enlightenment and for igniting the spark of clear and ready grasp in people you converse with, witness to, or lead. In short I believe this is an always-current, on-time book for end-time believers!

I encourage you to come to this book with a sense of the *critical need* for the truth it deals with; there is no greater theme than the blood of redemption's fountainhead! In an age when demonically inspired tales of werewolves and vampires are captivating multitudes, you can be sure: these are subtly designed distractions to either focus "blood" as related to superstitious tales or as a stimulus to relate it to the bizarre or the erotic or as fun ideas to speculate about. But when *the blood of Jesus Christ, the Lamb of God* is understood, and its weighty truth grasped and made functional in a person's heart and mind, you and I can enter a dimension of life where:

- Deeper devotion to Jesus and His love is experienced
- Greater equipping for life and ministry is received, and
- Bolder authority to confront the present darkness is exercised

I'm pleased and delighted *Signed in His Blood* is now in print and ready for use by all of us. We're the group I mentioned above, end-time believers, and we're the ones of whom the Book of Revelation prophesied. Speaking about us—the "Jesus people" of the last days—the Bible says:

> Then I heard a loud voice saying in heaven, "Now salvation, and strength, and the kingdom of our God, and the power of His Christ have come, for the accuser of our brethren, who accused them before our God day and night, has been cast down. And they overcame him by the blood of the Lamb and by the word of their testimony, and they did not love their lives to the death.

Therefore rejoice, O heavens, and you who dwell in them! Woe to the inhabitants of the earth and the sea! For the devil has come down to you, having great wrath, because he knows that he has a short time."

—REVELATION 12:10–12

Dear reader, we are the people privileged to live in the very moment of history declared here! There is every reason to be joyous, bold, and strong in the grace, truth, and victory of Christ's cross. This book will help move us all toward a firmer grasp and grip on the cross, its triumph, and our place to live, serve, lead, and triumph in its glory, light, and life! Read—and be blessed, emboldened, and equipped.

—JACK W. HAYFORD
CHANCELLOR, THE KING'S UNIVERSITY,
LOS ANGELES, CALIFORNIA
FOUNDER, THE CHURCH ON THE WAY, VAN NUYS, CALIFORNIA

There is a fountain filled with blood drawn from
   Emmanuel's veins;
And sinners plunged beneath that flood lose all their
   guilty stains.
Lose all their guilty stains, lose all their guilty stains;
And sinners plunged beneath that flood lose all their
   guilty stains.[1]

Preface

ONE OF THE most popular verses in Scripture begins with the words "For God so loved the world" (John 3:16). Could it really be that God loves us, especially when we consider all the sorrow and suffering in the world? How do we explain this love when humanity suffers so much pain? Why doesn't an all-powerful, loving God do more to stop the carnage? Where is He in the midst of a hurting world?

No topic other than the blood of Jesus can better help us understand the depth of God's love for humanity. I pray that by exploring this subject you will come to know the amazing power in Jesus's blood and the incredible hope we have through Christ.

Why Blood?

I DON'T LIKE SPOOKY things. Ghost stories and horror movies are not my taste. I'm not interested in blood, guts, and gore as entertainment. Paradoxically, however, I find the subject of blood to be quite interesting. It's the very element that gives us and nearly every other creature on earth life. But blood also carries deep spiritual significance.

Of all the themes in the Bible, blood is one of the most important. The Bible indicates that blood, specifically Jesus's blood:

- Establishes relationships with God
- Is the only means of receiving forgiveness for sin
- Opens the human heart to receive healing
- Closes the mouths of deceiving spirits
- Demolishes the doctrines of demons
- Energizes the human spirit
- Empowers us to resist sin
- Cleans up a bad conscience
- Gives meaning and direction to life
- Guarantees our entrance into God's presence
- Brings Jesus into focus

Why is there such power in this red substance? Many Christians know the blood of Jesus is vital to our salvation. They know that without the shedding of blood there is no remission of sin (Heb. 9:22) and no way for mankind to be brought back into fellowship with God. But there is more. Without blood there would be no covenant with God in the first place, because God has chosen to use blood to seal lasting agreements between Himself and the people He created. From the first drop shed when God slaughtered animals to make skins to cover Adam's and Eve's nakedness and their sin all the way to the new covenant, blood has allowed mankind to have a relationship with God. This crucial role blood plays in covenants with God makes it a powerful weapon in the unseen but a very real war going on in the heavens.

Like it or not, blood is a topic that cannot be ignored. My prayer is that this book provides a fresh understanding of the incredible, life-giving power of Jesus's blood. I hope it presents a more-than-casual overview of what the Bible teaches about blood and blood covenants and how applying that knowledge can help us live in deeper, more intimate communion with God, which is the very reason we exist.

CHAPTER 1

A Covenant of Blood

*And He has made from one blood every nation
of men to dwell on all the face of the earth.*

—Acts 17:26

Talk of blood is all around us. You've probably heard the sayings, "Blood is thicker than water," referring to the bond between blood relatives; or "blood in and blood out," noting gang initiation and exodus; or "in cold blood," relating to callous killings. Even "purple heart" is a reference to blood. It is clear that we are conscious of the fact that blood gives and sustains life, but this is not only true biologically. Blood is also just as vital to our spiritual life. A proper understanding of blood, especially the atoning power of Jesus's blood, is essential if as Christians we are to live a full and meaningful life and know how to overcome the enemy of our souls.

Blood shows up throughout Scripture, not only on the Old Testament battlefields but also as the bond that gives life to relationships. In fact, blood is called the scarlet thread of the Scriptures. Evangelist D. L. Moody said, "If you cut the crimson thread that binds the Bible, it falls to pieces."[1] It is Christ's blood that washes of us our sins (Rev. 1:5). It is His blood that purifies (Heb. 9:22), justifies (Rom. 5:9), and empowers us to serve God (Heb. 9:14). And it is by Jesus's blood that we have been reconciled to God (Col. 1:19–20).[2] Through the blood of Christ—not merely the death of Christ but specifically through His blood, as we will explore more fully in later chapters—God made peace between heaven and earth.

Preachers in every generation have understood the importance of blood for salvation. St. John Chrysostom called the blood of Jesus "the saviour of souls," St. Thomas Aquinas called it "the key to heaven's treasures," and St. Ambrose referred to it as "pure gold of ineffable worth."[3]

To quote theologian John Wesley, "Christian faith is then, not only an assent to the whole gospel of Christ, but also a full reliance on the blood of Christ; a trust in the merits of his life, death, and resurrection; a recumbency upon him as our atonement and our life, as given for us, and living in us; and, in consequence hereof, a closing with him, and cleaving to him, as our 'wisdom, righteousness, sanctification, and redemption,' or, in one word, our salvation."[4]

Not too many years ago Christians seemed to understand that blood was central to their relationship with God. Paging through old hymnals reveals a surprising number of songs about Jesus's blood. However, the subject of His blood is not reflected as much in songs sung in church today. Certainly many of the newer songs are a blessing to Christ's body, but somewhere along the line the emphasis on blood has been diminished. The question is, why? Why has blood, and especially Jesus's blood, been misplaced in Christian emphasis?

Because the emphasis on blood has been waning in the church, I believe we have lost sight of certain spiritual realities. Among the most important of these is the fact that God relates to humanity by way of covenant, and these covenants are always sealed in blood, symbolizing both the eternal nature of the covenant and the depth of intimacy God desires to have with mankind. One of my major motivations for writing this book is to reacquaint believers with the importance of blood to deepen the church's understanding of these truths.

THE PURPOSE OF BLOOD AND COVENANT

Most people know that blood sustains life, but many people do not realize that in most cultures blood has long been used to establish covenant relationships. Throughout much of the world blood historically has been the signature on lasting agreements. It represents the point at which an accord is sealed. Remember how kids used to become blood brothers in an attempt to cement their lives together forever? They would share some blood from a prick in a finger, and presto, they would be "blood brothers" or "blood sisters."

This concept originated in Scripture. God came up with this idea and called it "covenant." Today we actually refer to this as "blood covenant," because "blood" and "covenant" are so closely interwoven in the Scriptures that they can hardly be separated. And both are directly related to a clear understanding of biblical salvation.[5]

Because the concept of covenanting with a monotheistic God was first birthed among the Jewish people, I think it significant that respected Rabbi Harold Kushner writes that the most important word in the Torah after the name of God may very well be the word *brith*, which is usually translated "covenant."[6] Although the word *covenant* is used nearly three hundred times in Scripture, not much is said of it in modern times. Like blood, the church's emphasis on covenant either has been lost, misplaced, or purposely set aside over time. In this book we will take a close look at blood covenant in the Bible to understand the kind of relationship God desires to have with us and His plan for our redemption. We will explore each of the concepts below at length throughout this book, but I want to acquaint you with these seven key concepts related to the power of blood and covenant.

1. God establishes relationships with people only on the basis of a covenant.

"And as for Me, behold, I establish My covenant with you and with your descendants after you" (Gen. 9:9). In Scripture relationship with God is a lot like the marriage relationship in that bonding is essential to its function. A man and a woman connect through physical, mental, emotional, and spiritual intimacy initiated by a formal and binding marriage contract. The bond becomes so strong that it unites the two into a virtual oneness. A biblical relationship with God has many unique similarities to the marriage covenant.

2. Blood is used to form all covenants with God.

"Therefore not even the first covenant was dedicated without blood" (Heb. 9:18). This truth cannot be overlooked. God makes all lasting relationships with humanity only on the basis of blood. Covenants with Him are "signed" with blood (either literally as in the Old Testament or symbolically as in the New Testament) and made with the understanding that if they are ever broken, they are to be paid for in blood. Covenanting with God also implies not only His blessings and protection but also certain responsibilities mankind will fulfill.

In the Bible evidence of this kind of contractual relationship is revealed in bits and pieces that unquestionably point to blood covenants as the standard for making agreements with God. Scripture indicates that Adam was in covenant with God from the beginning of his existence. This is noted by the prophet Hosea: "But like Adam they transgressed the covenant; there they dealt faithlessly with me" (Hosea 6:7, ESV). A covenant must have existed in order for Adam to have transgressed it.

This is believed to have been a blood covenant because after it was broken by Adam and Eve's sin, God shed animals' blood to cover their nakedness. This along with the sacrifices offered by Noah after the flood, the more direct account of covenant making in the lives of Abraham and Moses, and the manner in which the new covenant was signed all point overwhelmingly to a single method for establishing a relationship with God—blood covenant.

Blood is the agent that binds heaven to earth. Scripture says, "But now in Christ Jesus you who once were far away have been brought near through the blood of Christ" (Eph. 2:13, NIV). Near to what or to whom? Near to God! Humanity can't get near to God in any way other than through blood, specifically Jesus's blood!

3. Blood covenant relationships with God go back to the beginning.

"This is My covenant which you shall keep, between Me and you and your descendants after you" (Gen. 17:10). The idea of covenanting with God goes back to the beginning of time—all the way back to Adam and Eve. All the eras, or dispensations,[7] of time are the same when it comes to getting to know God by way of a covenant. God covenants with people in every generation and in every age in exactly the same manner He has done from the beginning. Nothing ever changes in the way He makes agreements.

4. The New Testament reinforces blood covenant as God's way of establishing relationships.

"Likewise He also took the cup after supper, saying, 'This cup is the new covenant in My blood, which is shed for you'" (Luke 22:20). In comparing God's dealings with people on both sides of the cross, the principles and methods He uses are not just similar; they are identical. For instance, Passover and Communion are virtually the same, though Passover could be said to be a type or shadow of Communion. These two great observances are both memorials for blood covenants with God.[8] Also, physical circumcision in the old covenant is a picture of heart circumcision in the new covenant.

These kinds of parallels affirm that God does not change. They further declare that God establishes His covenants with people on the basis of His character. He doesn't change, and neither do His covenant stipulations. His moral laws are not rules thought up for individual situations or given uniquely for dispensations of progressive enlightenment. They are a direct reflection of who He is and are always the same no matter where they are observed in either the Old or New Testaments.

5. Blood is the ultimate weapon against the enemy of our souls.

"And they overcame him by the blood of the Lamb" (Rev. 12:11). While in exile on the Isle of Patmos, John received a revelation from Jesus. Among the many things revealed, he saw Christ's blood as a weapon for overcoming Satan and his demons, because it gives us authority over the enemy and releases us from satanic bondage and the power of sin. (See chapter 24.)

The fledgling church was in the process of gearing up for battle, one the likes of which the world had never seen. Quickly God shifted the focus of the early disciples from the natural realm to the spiritual. And just as quickly came the need to know how to fight in this new arena. John's Jewish background, no doubt, allowed him to easily transfer his knowledge of blood and covenant into an understanding of how the church could effectively wage spiritual warfare. It is clear in the New Testament that the early church's understanding of spiritual authority was void of enchantment and magic. To them spiritual warfare wasn't weird or nonsensical. It was a present and understandable reality for which spiritual weapons were of absolute necessity.

6. Blood is the only agent capable of cleansing sin.

"But if we walk in the light as He is in the light, we have fellowship with one another, and the blood of Jesus Christ His Son cleanses us from all sin" (1 John 1:7). Many people have experienced times when it seemed sin could never be removed from the fabric of a stained life. No amount of crying, remorse, or sorrow could erase it from a condemning memory. Only when they discovered in God's Word that Jesus's blood could wash away what no amount of begging, pleading, or good works could remove did they find any real peace.

Hebrews 9:22 sums it up: "And according to the law almost all things are purified with blood, and without shedding of blood there is no remission [forgiveness]." The shedding of

Jesus's blood is the only way our sin can be cleansed. There is no other way for this cleansing from sin to take place. A lack of understanding concerning the nature and power of Jesus's blood is one of the reasons some people can't seem to get rid of the memory of past sins. So powerful is this cleansing agent that once the process is complete, the sin is "as if it never happened."

7. God's ultimate goal is for us to rule and reign with Him throughout eternity.

"If we endure, we shall also reign with Him. If we deny Him, He also will deny us" (2 Tim. 2:12). In the Book of Revelation the romance of the ages concludes with a wedding. It is the point at which God permanently unites with His people. The late evangelist Paul Billheimer said that God is looking for an "eternal companion," a bride for the Lamb, someone to be at His side as He governs the universe.[9] (See Revelation 21:9.) Billheimer further explained that this present life is about training for rulership.[10] Although we may not see or perceive it clearly, God desires to have a very close relationship with us. This is the crux of the plan that He continues to work out in the earth. (See Hebrews 2:5–8.)

TO KNOW HIM

For many people, if God does in fact exist, He is distant, vague, and aloof. To them He remains a concept or a cosmic force but not a person with whom one can communicate or even relate. They would say that it is not possible to really know God. But Jesus taught otherwise. He spoke of a God with whom we could talk, One who wanted to be in a relationship as close as that of any parent and child (Matt. 6:9–13). He went so far as to use the word "Abba" ("Daddy") to communicate that Father God could actually be thought of as "Daddy God" (Gal. 4:6). The more Jesus speaks about a personal relationship with God, the more some hearts pound with a desire to respond. Something deep within the human frame yearns for more than a distant God.

But if relationships are to be developed and if fellowship is to be successful, there must be an understanding of the manner in which God allows humanity into His presence, and that manner involves blood. In the pages that follow we will explore why God uses blood covenants to establish relationship. But it is not enough to simply study and establish some good theological propositions and positions on a subject. We must be able to apply those truths to daily life. If there is not application, the knowledge is virtually useless. Therefore, in the pages that follow you will also find suggestions for applying truths revealed in the method God has chosen to unite with mankind.

CHAPTER 2

Life Is in the Blood

For the life of the flesh is in the blood.

—LEVITICUS 17:11

ALTHOUGH THE PURPOSE of this book is to examine the spiritual significance of blood, I want to take a moment to explore some of its physical characteristics. Some people believe life is in the heart or in the brain, but both science and Scripture indicate that life is in the blood.

The average human body contains about five to six quarts of blood flowing through as much as sixty thousand miles of veins and arteries in a cycle that takes less than thirty seconds to complete.[1] This process requires a tremendous amount of pressure exerted from a most amazing organ, the heart.

Blood consists basically of two elements, a liquid called plasma and cells called corpuscles. Other elements such as enzymes, proteins, and hormones are also present. Plasma is a colorless substance made up of about 90 percent water that carries the cells in its flow. As for our blood cells, three types are manufactured in the marrow of our bones: red and white blood cells, and platelets. These cells are the agents that nourish and protect the body.[2]

Red cells. Red cells (erythrocytes) are tiny round disks, about 0.003 of an inch in diameter, that carry oxygen to the tissue in our bodies and that carry waste products away. They are basically fuel cells that deliver life-sustaining oxygen to the right place at precisely the right moment. The average size person has about twenty-five trillion red blood cells. Each one of those cells has a life span of about four months, meaning that each day approximately two hundred billion cells die and have to be replaced. The idea that blood is blue and only turns red when exposed to oxygen is not true. Blood is red is because of a substance in each red cell called hemoglobin, which contains a quantity of iron.

White cells. White blood cells (leukocytes) defend the body against pollutants. When an infection or some other foreign substance is introduced into the body, these cells surround the intruder like soldiers on a battlefield and fight until it leaves. For example, when a cut or scrape on the skin develops a redness around it, this usually means that extra blood has gathered in that area to help in the healing process. The body contains about five hundred to one thousand times more red cells than white cells, but when an infection strikes, white cells are manufactured in larger numbers. If the body has trouble manufacturing white blood cells, it cannot defend itself against disease and could eventually die.

Platelets. Platelets (thrombocytes) are the smallest of the three kinds of blood cells and band together with proteins in the plasma to stop bleeding. They are like maintenance cells. When there is a leak in the dike these cells hurry to plug the hole. The blood system acts as an army: supply ships, soldiers, and maintenance teams all standing ready to keep an enemy invader from damaging the body.

Despite the many differences between the peoples of our world, there is virtually no difference in the blood from one person to another. The Bible tells us what science now confirms: "He has made from one blood every nation of men to dwell on all the face of the earth" (Acts 17:26). Other than minor variations in blood types, it doesn't matter where a person is born or the color of his or her skin; the blood is the same. What is most significantly different from one person to the next is our DNA.

Animal blood, on the other hand, is quite different from human blood, which is why it cannot be used in transfusions. This is yet another case of science confirming what the Bible teaches. First Corinthians 15:39 tells us, "All flesh is not the same flesh, but there is one kind of flesh of men, another flesh of animals, another of fish, and another of birds."

So much of our interest as humans has to do with understanding why we are here and how our lives are sustained. In this quest the Bible can again serve as a guide. From it we learn that life is not found in the brain, heart, or any other organ. Rather, "the life of the flesh is in the blood" (Lev. 17:11).

Because blood is the element that carries life, the Bible tells us it is sacred. When Noah departed the ark, God told him to be fruitful and multiply. He went on to say, "Every moving thing that lives shall be food for you.... But you shall not eat flesh with its life, that is, its blood" (Gen. 9:3–4).

This prohibition against eating blood was recognized even centuries later in the days of King Saul. After Israel had conquered the Philistines in battle, the people slaughtered sheep, oxen, and cattle and ate the blood with the flesh. A complaint soon came back to Saul: "Look, the people are sinning against the LORD by eating with the blood!" (1 Sam. 14:33).

The apostles too knew and respected this prohibition against consuming blood. Although certain customary Jewish restrictions were removed after Christ died and rose again, the early church was still instructed not to consume blood. "For it seemed good to the Holy Spirit, and to us, to lay upon you no greater burden than these necessary things: that you abstain from things offered to idols, *from blood*, from things strangled, and from sexual immorality. If you keep yourselves from these, you will do well" (Acts 15:28–29, emphasis added).

More than two thousand years later, life is still in the blood, and blood is still sacred.

CHAPTER 3

The Source of Life and Peace

*For it pleased the Father that in Him [Jesus] all the
fullness should dwell, and by Him to reconcile all things
to Himself, by Him, whether things on earth or things in
heaven, having made peace through the blood of His cross.*

—COLOSSIANS 1:19–20

SECULAR HISTORIANS OFTEN overlook the biblical record
and the people of faith in the unfolding drama of human
history. This is especially true when it comes to examining spiritual dynamics shadowing our present world. When a secular
person writes about war and conflict, they almost never tell
of any spiritual influences behind the struggle. Satan and his
demons are rarely recognized for the role they play in the problems of humanity.

Behind the Napoleons, the Alexander the Greats, and even
the Hitlers of the world are spiritual forces that affect the
course of history. We do not only wrestle with flesh and blood,
but we also war with principalities and powers, with the rulers
of the darkness of this world and spiritual wickedness in high
places (Eph. 6:12–18). And at the core of this struggle is one
thing: blood.

The popularity of the movie *The Passion of the Christ* has
increased public awareness of the uniqueness of Jesus's blood.
But many still don't actually understand how Christ's blood
brings salvation, peace, and purpose in life. It is one of the
greatest of human tragedies that so many lack knowledge of
the importance of His blood.

Easter's message of the resurrection of Christ is preceded

by the crucifixion, an act that was bathed in blood. It's easy to miss the fullness of the power of Easter by focusing only on the beauty of the Resurrection and overlooking the brutality of the cross. Jesus wanted us to remember His blood. That is why we drink the cup at Communion. At the Last Supper, which was the first Communion, Jesus said, "This is My blood of the new covenant, which is shed for many for the remission [forgiveness] of sins" (Matt. 26:28). Undoubtedly many have partaken of the Communion elements without truly understanding what the bread and cup represent.

THE BENEFITS OF CHRIST'S BLOOD

As we explore blood covenants, it will become clear that only Christ's blood could redeem us from the power of sin and death. We will also see why His blood is a key weapon in our war against the enemy. But before we look at why Jesus's blood is so powerful, I want to focus on what it accomplishes for mankind.

Jesus's blood reconciles us to God.

"But now in Christ Jesus you who once were far off have been brought near by the blood of Christ" (Eph. 2:13). The Scriptures teach that Jesus's blood reestablishes our relationship (or reconciles us) to God.

Jesus's blood covers all the wrong a person has ever done.

"In Him we have redemption through His blood, the forgiveness of sins, according to the riches of His grace" (Eph. 1:7). The apparent tragedy of the cross resulted in ultimate good—the forgiveness of sins. Redemption carries with it the idea of Jesus "buying back" humanity and delivering us from enslavement to sin.

Jesus's blood keeps a person free from sin.

"But if we walk in the light as He is in the light, we have fellowship with one another, and the blood of Jesus Christ His Son cleanses us from all sin" (1 John 1:7). Few things in life are as troubling as the guilt and condemnation of sin. Even after accepting Christ, some people just can't get the past out of their minds. They think, "If only I hadn't done this or that. How could I have been so stupid? Why didn't I listen?" To say we have been "washed in the blood" is not to use a quaint religious phrase to pacify those chained to their past. It is to declare a truth that has the power to release a person from guilt and condemnation. When we accept Christ, we are truly cleansed, and He no longer sees us cloaked in the mistakes of our past. Rather, He sees us with robes that are washed and made white in the blood of the Lamb (Rev. 7:13–14). He wants us to see ourselves that way too so we can walk in the fullness of our authority in Him, but I will talk more about that in later chapters.

Jesus's blood sanctifies us.

"Therefore Jesus also, that He might sanctify the people with His own blood, suffered outside the gate" (Heb. 13:12). Sanctification means "to be set apart," and the application of Jesus's blood sets a person apart as God's very own. The Creator of the universe is looking for people to call His own; in fact, the King of heaven has issued a personal invitation to us to join Him at His throne. Jesus's blood not only sets people apart for God's purposes but also empowers them to stand against the enemy, who would keep them from accepting the invitation.

Jesus's blood gives us access to God's presence.

"Therefore, brethren, having boldness to enter the Holiest by the blood of Jesus" (Heb. 10:19). Blaise Pascal, the French physicist and philosopher, spoke of a "God-shaped vacuum" in every human being that only God Himself can fill. Mankind lost the glory, or presence of God, in his life when sin entered the world (Gen. 3). Reconciliation can restore that lost glory and give us access to God's presence, but that restoration and access come only through Jesus's blood.

Jesus's blood justifies the guilty.

"Being justified freely by His grace through the redemption that is in Christ Jesus" (Rom. 3:24). One of the common ways the enemy likes to attack us is through accusation. Scripture actually refers to Satan as the accuser of God's people (Rev. 12:10). When the words "and you call yourself a Christian" come to mind, often they have been planted by the enemy to make us feel condemned for not living up to God's standards. Without a proper understanding of justification, we can get stuck there, thinking we have failed God and that He is angry with us. Once sin is dealt with through Christ, in a very real sense it is "as if it never happened." It is gone forever, never to be acknowledged again. That is what it means to be justified. When we sin, we must repent, and God is faithful to forgive us. But our good works before God don't justify us, as Satan would like us to think. Nothing we do or don't do can make us right before God; we are justified only by Jesus's blood.

Jesus's blood cleanses a defiled conscience.

"How much more shall the blood of Christ, who through the eternal Spirit offered Himself without spot to God, cleanse your conscience from dead works to serve the living God?" (Heb. 9:14). Many people pursue religious activities in order to appease God or their own conscience. They think they must somehow pay Him back for the wrongs they have done, or even that they need to earn the right to enter heaven. Intuitively we all sense that something is wrong in our lives and needs to be made right. Almost everyone comes to a point where they look for something to rid them of the guilt they feel. They wonder, "How much good do I have to do to make up for the bad that is making me feel so miserable?"

This is where Christianity differs from other religions. Christianity teaches that the solution to human misery and enmity with God is found only in a relationship with God through Christ, and the only thing necessary to establish that relationship is to receive Jesus (John 1:12). Other religions usually promote a spiritual to-do list that will make a person acceptable to God. Our God doesn't require us to be good first in order to come to Him.

The Bible says, "But when the kindness and the love of God our Savior toward man appeared, not by works of righteousness which we have done, but according to His mercy He saved us, through the washing of regeneration and renewing of the Holy Spirit, whom He poured out on us abundantly through Jesus Christ our Savior, that having been justified by His grace we should become heirs according to the hope of eternal life" (Titus 3:4–7). Christianity is God reaching down to man. All other religions stress the need to not only reach up to God but also to make sure we have something in our hands to offer Him.

Jesus's blood brings peace to troubled hearts.

At Jesus's birth the heavenly hosts promised peace to men (Luke 2:14). In one way or another everyone is looking for peace. The Scriptures declare that genuine and lasting peace is available only through Jesus's blood, "Having made peace through the blood of His cross..." (Col. 1:19–20).

It is easy to assume that it's too difficult to comprehend the value of Jesus's blood and so do virtually nothing to grasp its meaning. That thinking has disastrous results. It is like a homeless man who received a rich relative's last will and testament. The will provided him a large home, land, money, servants, and great authority, but because he didn't understand the document, the inheritance lay unclaimed for the rest of the man's life.

That really is the picture of people who read the Bible but fail to comprehend the significance of Jesus's blood. Everything we need for life and godliness is found in Christ through His blood. When we struggle through life feeling ashamed and condemned about our past, or uncertain of whether Jesus really loves us, or thinking we have to earn God's favor or the right to enter into His presence, we live far beneath our inheritance as children of God. How true are the prophet Hosea's words, "My people are destroyed for lack of knowledge" (Hosea 4:6).

AN UNSEEN WAR

While the Scriptures emphasize that Jesus's blood is required for salvation and cleansing from sin, many Christians don't like to focus on Jesus's blood, worrying that Christianity will be seen as a "bloody religion." Some have gone so far as to demand that songs containing references to blood be removed from their hymnals. Any kind of biblical ignorance, including this, can be detrimental to one's spiritual life and leave a person open to satanic attack. Take away the emphasis on Jesus's blood, and you have no basis for a relationship with God and no means for resisting Satan and his demons.

The New Testament is a series of books about a war, one currently being waged in both the spiritual and natural realms and fought only according to biblical principles. At first the apostle Peter thought this war was earthly and physical. He even carried a sword while following Jesus. Evidently Peter initially believed that the Messiah had come to liberate Jerusalem from oppressive Roman rule. But by the Day of Pentecost he understood something far more complex—that there was an unseen war going on in the heavenlies. Some years later, and with much greater understanding, Peter cautioned the church, "Be sober, be vigilant; because your adversary the devil walks about like a roaring lion, seeking whom he may devour" (1 Pet. 5:8).

Many Christians today who trust the Bible also believe that there is a spiritual battle under way. They know they fight through prayer and praise and that the outcomes of spiritual battles affect the natural realm. They also will tell you that many of these battles cannot be won without calling upon the power that is ours through Jesus's blood. These Christians realize that Christ has given His people authority over demons, as Luke 10:19 states. Yet they also realize that they cannot act in their own strength; they must operate in Jesus's authority by partnering with Jesus through His blood (Matt. 28:18).

Scripture makes it clear that Jesus's blood gives us power and authority to war against the enemy of the human soul. Satan and his demons know that Christ's blood is devastating to their cause. The devil knows the end of the story, declared in Revelation 12:11: "And they overcame him by the blood of the Lamb and by the word of their testimony." Demons hate the blood of the Lamb and fear the person who understands how to appropriate it. But they rejoice when the blood is ignored. A bloodless Christianity is no threat to the enemy.

Calvary not only represents release from sin, but it also represents Satan's defeat by way of Christ's blood. This is why the church must preach and sing of His blood. There are numerous passages in the New Testament that speak of resisting or confronting the enemy (James 4:7; 2 Cor. 2:11; Eph. 4:27; 6:10–12), and Jesus's blood is a key weapon that enables us to overcome.

DEAD IN SIN, ALIVE IN CHRIST

The power of Christ's blood to free us from the bondage of sin is no small matter. Medical advances have done well to keep people alive much longer than in past eras. At the turn of the last century the average life expectancy in the United States was around fifty years old. Today, because of medicines and disease-fighting strategies, it is closer to the age of eighty.[1] People want to extend their lives, so science continues to look for the proverbial "fountain of youth." But from a scriptural standpoint the issue is much more complex.

Dying has more to do with the inner spiritual condition of human beings than with the problems associated with aging. Romans 5:12 says, "Therefore, just as through one man sin entered the world, and death through sin, and thus death spread to all men, because all sinned." Even if we could perfect all of our food, air, and water, the biblical implication is that sin would still cause human bodies to die. We die because of sin.

That is why sin must be dealt with if we are to be redeemed. Many people believe they can take care of sin by not sinning. Not so! Only Jesus can deal with our nature, which has been infused with sin.

The connection between sin and death goes back to the Garden of Eden. In Genesis 2 God told Adam, "Of every tree of the garden you may freely eat; but of the tree of the knowledge of good and evil you shall not eat, for in the day that you eat of it you shall surely die" (vv. 15–17). When Adam and Eve disobeyed God in the garden, sin entered the world and brought with it death. I believe that since life is in the blood and death overtakes life as a result of sin, sin must have infected our blood, because every generation since Adam has been plagued by the same sin sickness that leads to spiritual and physical death. The cure, then, for this spiritual disease is found in a person whose blood was pure in every sense of the word. Jesus could triumph over sin because He had no sin within Himself to bring about death. Since death entered Adam and his bloodline because he was sinful, only someone without sin in His life could regenerate those descended from Adam and therefore born with a nature infused with sin.

This is why the virgin birth is exceedingly important. For Jesus to be the kind of Savior the Bible describes, He would have had to be spiritually and physically uncontaminated by sin. The fact that humanity was born in sin and conceived in iniquity (Ps. 51:5) prevents the Savior of humanity from being conceived through normal means. If Joseph were Jesus's biological father, Christ would have been fully human and tainted with sin. Only a unique conception would enable a sinless man to walk among us and win the spiritual battle over sin that would forever reconcile humanity to God. Hence, the virgin birth.

Just as a point of clarity, the fact that Jesus was without sin does not mean Mary was sinless. The mother of Jesus needed a savior just like the rest of humanity. There is, however, some debate about whether her blood coursed through Jesus's veins.

I recommend you review my comments in the notes section for a summary of four views on that matter.[2] Amid all the debates, there is one crucial thing for us to remember: Jesus was fully man and fully God. He was flesh and blood (Heb. 2:14), tempted in every way we are, yet He was without sin. And with that sinless blood Jesus redeemed all of humanity from the scourge of sin and death.

A new spiritual life begins when we are reconciled to God and His Spirit comes to live within us. When we are redeemed by the blood of Jesus, we become new creatures. "Old things have passed away; behold, all things have become new" (2 Cor. 5:17). This is why Christianity is not a mind-set, a list of dos and don'ts, a legalistic lifestyle, or a church. Christianity is literally a matter of being "in Christ" (Col. 1:28) and the subsequent miracle of Christ being in us by the Holy Spirit (Col. 1:27; Gal. 2:20).

JESUS *IS* LIFE

"When Christ who is our life appears, then you also will appear with Him in glory" (Col. 3:4). Many people enjoy mysteries—not the ones filled with blood and guts but good, old-fashioned whodunits that require some imagination and ingenuity to figure things out. Paul writes about a mystery that he says was hidden from generations past but now is available for us to understand. The mystery? Christ in us! The true power of Christianity is literally Christ by His Spirit living within a body of believers as well as in the individual believer. The Bible tells us: "And so it is written, 'The first man Adam became a living being.' The last Adam [Jesus] became a life-giving spirit" (1 Cor. 15:45). And again, "This is the testimony: that God has given us eternal life, and this life is in His Son. He who has the Son has life; he who does not have the Son of God does not have life" (1 John 5:11–12).

This life of "Christ in us" happens through the Holy Spirit, whom Jesus sent when He ascended into heaven (Col. 1:24–27).

As important as holy living is, few things are more dangerous to spiritual vitality than the belief that Christianity is defined by good living. Righteousness and holiness coming through Jesus are important and necessary, but it is not possible to live this righteous lifestyle without the life of Christ operating from within us. Scripture says, "It is God who works in you both to will and to do for His good pleasure" (Phil. 2:13).

"Christ in you, the hope of glory" (Col. 1:27) takes on a deeper and more practical meaning when we see that Jesus sustains and nourishes our spirits in the same way food nourishes our physical bodies. Jesus is "the way, the truth, and *the life*" (John 14:6, emphasis added). Paul spoke of the "life of Jesus" being "manifested in our body" and "in our mortal flesh" (2 Cor. 4:10–11). Andrew Murray describes the relationship between the flesh and the life of Jesus in the following way:

> By sin, a middle wall of partition separated God and man. "The flesh" was the veil that made true union impossible. As long as sin was not atoned for, God, by His Spirit, could not take up a settled abode in the heart of man. Until the power of the flesh was broken and subdued, the Spirit could not manifest His authority. For this reason, there is no mention in the days of the Old Testament of an outpouring of the Spirit of God except as a prediction of what should be in the last days. Also our Lord Jesus was not in a position to bestow upon His disciples the Spirit with whom He had been baptized, even though He took them into the closest fellowship with Himself, though He greatly loved them and longed to bless them....
>
> What man himself could not do, that the Lord Jesus, the Son of Man, did for him. He shed His blood. He gave His life in entire surrender to the will of God as a satisfaction of the penalty of sin. When that was accomplished, it was possible for Him to receive the Spirit from the Father that He might pour Him out. The outpouring of the blood rendered possible the outpouring of the Spirit.

This is declared in the Scriptures in such words as these: "The Spirit was not yet given, because Jesus was not yet glorified" (John 7:39).[3]

The power of sin in a person remains unchecked until the Spirit of God enters him personally. And again, when Christ comes to a person, He deals first with the problem of sin. When Christianity deteriorates, it does so almost always by emphasizing new lifestyles without directing the focus to the only person who can change those lifestyles. Even an emphasis on discipleship can be deadly if it is not preceded by an emphasis on Christ's ability to transform through the Holy Spirit. One falls easily into self-righteousness when he tries to live properly in his own strength.

Perhaps no scripture emphasizes the life found in Jesus as much as John 6:51: "I am the living bread which came down from heaven. If anyone eats of this bread, he will live forever; and the bread that I shall give is My flesh, which I shall give for the life of the world." Also worth noting are John 5:21 and 26: "For as the Father raises the dead and gives life to them, even so the Son gives life to whom He will.... For as the Father has life in Himself, so He has granted the Son to have life in Himself."

Make no mistake, this "life" spoken of in the Scriptures is not merely the "force" behind human existence. This life is God's presence for which we were created and by which we are to be energized and sustained. Our bodies have life in them but not the sustaining life that God originally intended. Romans 8:11 says, "But if the Spirit of Him who raised Jesus from the dead dwells in you, He who raised Christ from the dead will also give life to your mortal bodies through His Spirit who dwells in you." Certainly this verse implies that God will eventually transform fleshly bodies into new and gloriously incorruptible ones. But there is another dynamic that must not be missed—that the Holy Spirit who now indwells a person who has accepted Jesus is giving that person immortal "life." As

Ephesians 2:1 says, "And you He made alive, who were dead in trespasses and sins."

Indeed, Christianity is the very life of God flowing from within a believer to ultimately result in personal decisions that produce a godly lifestyle. Christ's life within the human frame fosters oneness with God, and it is this unity with God that brings change. Bible teacher Paul Billheimer sums it up well:

> Through the new birth we become bona fide members of the original cosmic family (Ephesians 3:15), actual generated sons of God (1 John 3:2), "partakers of the divine nature" (2 Peter 1:4), begotten by Him, impregnated with His "genes",* called the seed or "sperma" of God (1 John 5:1, 18 and 1 Peter 1:3, 23), and bearing His heredity. Thus, through the new birth—and I speak reverently—we become the "next of kin" to the Trinity, a kind of extension of the Godhead.... Here is a completely new, unique, and exclusive order of beings which may be called a "new species." *There is nothing like it in all the kingdoms of infinity.* This is the order of beings which God envisioned when He spoke the worlds into being. This is the order of beings which Paul called "the new man" (Ephesians 2:15), the "new humanity" destined through the new birth to be the aristocracy of the universe.
> *No physical relationship is implied.[4]

In his excellent book *Intercessory Prayer* Dutch Sheets shares an additional insight: "He [God] has now made His throne in our hearts and we are the temple of the Holy Spirit. We are the *naos* of God. In 1 Corinthians 3:16 and 6:19 this word means, 'holy of holies.' We are now the holy of holies, the dwelling place of God upon the earth. When He moves to release power upon the earth, it doesn't have to shoot out of the sky somewhere—it comes from His people where His Spirit dwells upon the earth."[5]

APPLYING CHRIST'S BLOOD

With Christ living in us and working through us, we can avert many of life's difficulties if we know how to apply Christ's blood in our lives. All that we know and understand about blood, especially Jesus's blood, has little meaning if it is not applied. Without application all of the preceding information about His blood serves no real purpose. Unless there is more than a cursory understanding of His blood, there is no real basis for the release of spiritual power.

How, then, is the blood applied to a person's life? It all begins by receiving Jesus. "But as many as received Him, to them He gave the right to become children of God, to those who believe in His name" (John 1:12). This simple beginning literally opens a dialogue with heaven to begin the reconciliation and restoration process.

At this point the benefits of being washed in Jesus's blood begin to take effect. First, a covenantal contract (literally a blood covenant) is signed and our names are recorded in the Lamb's Book of Life (Rev. 21:27), which stands as a legal document securing our place in heaven. Meanwhile Jesus becomes our advocate, or attorney (1 John 2:1–2; Heb. 7:25), and defends us against all outstanding warrants and accusations on the basis that our wrongs have been cleansed by His blood.

Jesus's blood not only provides forgiveness and release from sin, but it also bridges the gap that separates all human beings from God. It provides lasting reconciliation and friendship with Him. Again, so complete is this forgiveness that in God's eyes it is as if the wrongdoing never happened. The Bible says, "As far as the east is from the west, so far has He removed our transgressions from us" (Ps. 103:12). And, "If we confess our sins, He is faithful and just to forgive us our sins and to cleanse us from all unrighteousness" (1 John 1:9). Jesus's blood accomplished a permanent blow to sin, but His blood cannot do anything in us until it is personally applied. Again, that begins when we humbly submit to and receive Jesus.

"PLEADING" THE BLOOD

Before I close this chapter I want to touch briefly on another way we apply Jesus's blood in our lives as a weapon in spiritual warfare. (We will look more carefully at this in chapter 19.) We apply Jesus's blood in our lives as we "call" upon it. Proclaiming "I plead the blood of Jesus" can unleash God's power during times of spiritual trouble, especially demonic attack. When we plead the blood of Jesus, we are telling demonic spirits that they cannot control us because Jesus triumphed over them when He shed His blood on the cross.

Amazing results, including healings and deliverances, have occurred in response to earnest pleas for Christ's power to be brought to bear on a specific situation. People involved in spiritual warfare know firsthand that demons hate Jesus's blood. Mentioning the blood immediately applies the power of the living Christ to the problem. And no demon can stand against the power of God. For this reason the devil hates the blood; mention it and demons react.

We could say we *appeal*, *beseech*, *ask for*, or *petition* the blood of Jesus, and we'd still get the same results. Regardless of the term we use, when we call on the blood of Jesus in prayer, we are essentially saying, "Father God, I want the life of Jesus, the life that is in His blood, to invade this circumstance." And His blood can do what we could never do for ourselves.

It is important to note that when we pray, "I plead the blood of Jesus," we are not tapping into some mystical or magical power. We are accessing the power (authority) available to God's covenant people. Through the blood of Jesus we have the authority to trample on serpents and scorpions, and over all the power of the enemy, and nothing shall by any means hurt us (Luke 10:19). Try it! The next time you face some kind of spiritual oppression or opposition, mention Jesus's blood. The next time temptation strikes, speak of His blood. This leads the way to deliverance and freedom.

As Andrew Murray writes, "Where the blood is honored,

preached, and believed in as the power of full redemption, there the way is opened for the fullness of the Spirit's blessing. And in proportion as the Holy Spirit truly works in the hearts of man, He leads them to glory in the blood of the Lamb."[6]

CHAPTER 4

Relationship by Agreement

"Come now, and let us reason together," says the LORD.

—ISAIAH 1:18

IN SEPARATE INSTANCES two anguished mothers struggled with deep concerns over sons whose hearts had become hardened against God. In both cases the sons had prayed for something they didn't readily receive, and as a result each decided not to follow God. In reality both sons were saying, "God, I'll serve You if You answer my prayer." God wanted to answer their prayers; we can be sure of that. But why didn't He?

What sometimes appears to be unanswered prayer is no small dilemma to many people. Much of the problem is centered on the belief that prayer is simply asking God for things, which often reduces the Creator of the universe to a divine gift giver. But prayer involves much more than just asking for things. It is a communication system designed to establish and develop a relationship with God. While Jesus made it clear that in the Father's house His children could "ask" for things, prayer must always be recognized as a dialogue intended to build a close personal relationship with God, not merely to receive the items on a wish list.

Jesus spoke of the requirements for answered prayer in John 15:7. "If you abide in Me, and My words abide in you, you will ask what you desire, and it shall be done for you." In essence God declares, "I'm obligated to answer only those who are in a relationship with Me. First, covenant with Me and then we will talk." God promises to bless and protect. But we have access to those benefits only when we are in covenant with the

Father, and the way to get to Him is through His Son, Jesus Christ (Acts 4:12).

On the flipside, if we are not in covenant with God, we are in league with the devil. First John 5:19 says, "We know that we are of God, and the whole world lies under the sway of the wicked one." And Jesus told the Pharisees in the Gospel of John, "You are of your father the devil, and the desires of your father you want to do. He was a murderer from the beginning, and does not stand in the truth, because there is no truth in him. When he speaks a lie, he speaks from his own resources, for he is a liar and the father of it" (John 8:44).

These are hard and sobering words, but the fact remains. Either a person belongs to the kingdom of light and life or to the kingdom of death and darkness (Col. 1:13). This is a reality that is best summed up in the words of Jesus: "He who is not with Me is against Me, and he who does not gather with Me scatters abroad" (Matt. 12:30). If we are neither hot nor cold, He will spew us right out of His mouth (Rev. 3:16).

COMING INTO AGREEMENT

Nearly everything we do in life is based on some kind of consent, often in the form of an agreement. Payment plans generally require a signed contract. Marriage is entered into by way of a legal document. In other matters a person might not always personally sign a form describing what they will or will not do, but by their actions they agree to certain rules and codes of conduct. For instance, by getting into a car and driving down the road, we are agreeing to abide by rules for safe driving if we want to avoid being penalized.

Agreements with stipulations form the basis for all rightful associations within a society. In much the same way a relationship with God is based on a type of binding agreement. God has used covenant to enter into relationship with humanity from the beginning of time. There is no other way for people to relate to Him. This fact is well established by the more than two hundred fifty times the Old Testament uses the Hebrew word *brith* (also spelled *beriyth*), which is translated "covenant." Two Hebrew words help us understand the power and depth of agreements made with God. The first is *karat*, which means "to cut." The second, mentioned above, is *brith*, or "covenant." Together they mean "to cut a covenant." Through the comingling of blood, either figuratively or literally, an agreement of love and respect is established that provides blessing and protection. As we will see in upcoming chapters, these two Hebrew words give new meaning to the phrase "cutting a deal."

Covenant agreements are the means by which God unites humanity to Himself. As British Bible teacher Arthur Pink explains, "God's dealings with men are all based upon His covenant engagements with them—He promising certain blessings upon their fulfillment of certain conditions."[1] God intends that we have a crystal-clear understanding of the *contractual* aspects of our relationship with Him, not only to hold us accountable but also so that we might more fully appreciate the incredible benefits of that covenant, which include His blessing and protection.

Of course, if we are in covenant with God, it's important that we know the provisions and requirements of that agreement. Are the terms mutually agreed upon, or does God simply tell us what to do? God could choose to relate to us as a dictator, but Scripture shows He has chosen not to do so.

Disputes over the word *brith* ("covenant") often center on the question of whether the meaning suggests a "mutual agreement" or a "unilateral decree." Under a mutual agreement both parties work to fulfill their responsibilities in order to maintain the relationship. Under a unilateral (one-sided) decree the submissive party labors to appease the other party in order to receive what was promised. The question before us is, does God's covenant with us contain some degree of mutuality? If so, how much? To what extent is mankind allowed to choose?

Some scholars, such as Leon Morris, view the God-man

covenant as "sovereign only." That is, God establishes the terms and man either agrees or disagrees. For example, Morris states that in Exodus 24 God chose the Israelites to be His people and then imposed certain rules on them. Their choice in the matter was whether to obey.[2] That is a reasonable biblical interpretation, but there is more to it. Morris's explanation makes it seems as though God couldn't care less what we think. It's as if He says, "I'm God. This is the deal. You can take it or leave it." Psalm 34:8 instructs us to "taste and see that the LORD is good." This suggests that God has a much more loving disposition and that while He would never do anything contrary to His nature, He might say, "Let's talk" (see Isaiah 1:18), because He wants the communion to bring us closer to Him.

Numerous scriptures suggest that God wants a close relationship with us, but it is difficult to imagine that God would ever request our input before instituting terms for a covenant agreement. What He does instead is invite us to choose whether we will covenant with Him in the first place. In other words, the covenant is essentially two-sided. We choose whether to enter into relationship with Him knowing obedience is part of that covenant relationship.

God says, "Come now, and let us reason together...though your sins are like scarlet, they shall be as white as snow; though they are red like crimson, they shall be as wool" (Isa. 1:18). By calling us to enter into covenant with Him, God is inviting us to choose for ourselves whom we will serve (Josh. 24:15). Thus there is both an element of sovereignty and mutuality involved in God's covenant with mankind. He is saying to His creation, "Choose Me so you can have a relationship with Me."

The stipulations within the covenant do not have to be fully mutual to make this a two-sided agreement. For humanity to help God draw up the conditions of our covenant relationship with Him would be ludicrous. If God can be trusted at all, then He can be trusted to put the agreement together correctly. After all, He is the one who established the order around which the spiritual and natural worlds are framed. He is the one whose sacrifice made a relationship with Him possible in the first place. We must trust God on this very basic level if we are to have any kind of relationship with Him.

This was exactly the case with Abraham. The Bible tells us that Abraham "believed in the LORD, and He accounted it to him for righteousness" (Gen. 15:6). While some might argue that there is nothing in Scripture to indicate that God chose certain people because they agreed to carry out His commands, it is quite possible that God chose Abraham only because of his willingness to establish a relationship that would eventually lead to obeying the conditions of a covenant.

THE GIFT OF FREE WILL

God gave us the gift of free will to establish a relationship that would eventually lead to obeying the conditions of a covenant. The problem with one-sided covenants is that, for the most part, they violate free will. If our relationship with God were truly one-sided and we did not have the ability to exercise free will, that would mean the suffering and sorrow in the world was all sanctioned and induced by God. Such thinking makes God the creator of evil and diminishes our responsibility for the choices we make. It is a fatalistic system that produces hopelessness, despair, and a casual attitude toward sin.

If mankind has no say in whether he will enter a covenant relationship with God, the covenant is unilateral. A unilateral, or one-sided, system typically regards the opinions, ideas, needs, and desires of the second party as unimportant. Love, admiration, and friendship are virtually impossible between the parties involved in such a covenant. If the church is to be, as Paul Billheimer says, "the Eternal Companion of the God-Man,"[3] that will require some sort of dialogue with God that goes beyond simply taking orders from Him.

To further verify that God wants to relate to people on the basis of agreement and not dictatorship, consider for a moment the two major divisions of the Bible—the Old and New Testaments. A testament is, in reality, a part of a covenant or agreement. In fact, the Old and New Testaments could be called the Old Agreement and the New Agreement, because a testament is not the covenant itself.

The Jewish people, who were guardians of the Old Testament law and the first recipients of the New Testament gospel, recognized that a covenant was an agreement. It could well be that Peter's assurance that he would not deny Jesus at the Last Supper was based on his understanding as a Jewish man of the seriousness of the blood covenant he entered into when he broke the bread and drank the cup with Jesus in the Upper Room. (This cutting of the new covenant is further explained in chapter 14.)

It may sound strange that God would form a relationship with people on the basis of a contract, especially since God has ultimate power and control over all of creation. What would possess an omnipotent God to form a bond with fallen humanity through what appears to be, at least in part, a give-and-take arrangement?[4] The answer is not an easy one, but it comes from Scripture and from human experience, and it begins with understanding free will.

C. S. Lewis noted that "free will, though it makes evil possible, is also the only thing that makes possible any love or goodness or joy worth having.... The happiness which God designs for His higher creatures is the happiness of being freely, voluntarily united to Him and to each other in an ecstasy of love and delight compared with which the most rapturous love between a man and woman on this earth is mere milk and water. And for that they must be free."[5]

In short, God says, "Come unto Me." Then He gives us a choice. We can accept Him or reject Him.

God's commandments may seem like demands, but God does not try to manipulate or control us as a dictator would. His rules are designed to keep us from harm. He knows what works and what doesn't better than we do because He made the universe.

God has no desire to take away our free will. Our unique personality and character hinge on it. Take away a person's ability to choose, and he is reduced to an emotionless, thoughtless hunk of protoplasm. Friendship, parenthood, creativity, and love would have no meaning. Life as we know it could not exist without the God-given gift called free will.

The fact that we have a free will does not in any way mitigate or diminish God's sovereignty. No creature will ever usurp the Creator's sovereign will. Furthermore, I realize that the subject of mutuality can be lost in how it is defined. I do not see, in any way, shape, or form, mankind coming to God and asking to enter into an agreement with Him. In fact, I don't see mankind coming to God in any sense of the word at all. It is always God coming to us. My argument that there is mutuality in our covenant with God is based only on the way the Bible characterizes our unique relationship with Him—as something similar to marital relationships.

Ephesians 5 describes Christ as the head of the church just as the husband is the head of the wife (v. 23), and in the Book of Revelation the church is described as Christ's bride (Rev. 19:7). If God's true intent in creating mankind was to provide a wife for the Son, a bride for the Lamb, a coequal to rule and reign with Him over the universe for eternity, then that bride would almost certainly have a say in the relationship. God's master plan was to draw mankind into a close intimacy with Him, not to lord over him. God is omnipotent, omnipresent, and omniscient. He could control us any day of the week if He so chose. But He doesn't want that kind of relationship with humanity.

Our relationship with God is one that we were specifically created for and one that far surpasses a servant-master association. Sadly many people think God wants to lord over us, and that misconception keeps them from drawing near to Him.

Satan knows this well, which is why he uses these misconstrued ideas about God to his own destructive ends.

MUTUAL CONSENT

When it comes to salvation, God first draws us to Himself; He makes the first overture, then we must decide whether or not to accept His invitation. And once we have exercised our free will in this decision process, we can begin to fellowship with Him. What kind of relationship could we possibly have with God if we had no will to exercise? Free will requires permission in order for fellowship to take place. Simply put, if God wants to commune with someone, He needs that person's consent.

Certainly we have no bargaining power with God. We were born in sin, and God hates sin. Yet He allows mankind to choose whether to have a relationship with Him. In the Old Testament God often pleaded with His people to return to Him when He could have easily demanded their allegiance. One word from an all-powerful God and all of humanity would lie prostrate before Him. But what would forced loyalty accomplish? Certainly not mutual love, admiration, and respect. Therefore, God created covenant to serve as a door to a two-sided relationship with humanity.

Some scholars suggest that covenants with God are "suzerain-vassal" or "lord-vassal" in nature. A suzerain was a king or lord in the Near East. The vassal was subservient to the suzerain. This type of treaty was seen among the Hittites as early as the fourteenth century BC and among the Assyrians around the seventh century BC. The treaties were called "suzerainty treaties," and the relationships were not mutual. The suzerain made the stipulations, and the vassal agreed or was forced to carry them out. It has been argued that God's covenants in the Old Testament were like this, that God showed Himself to be the Great Suzerain. But it is unlikely that God would model His relationship with mankind after any earthly ruling system. On the contrary, at best these nations were practicing a distorted form of the divine covenant already in existence.[6]

Ancient suzerain-vassal treaties often contained part or all of the following:

- A preamble identifying the parties involved
- A historical prologue acknowledging previous relations
- The stipulations and demands of the suzerain
- The swearing of the oath
- Witnesses to the oath[7]

Those who subscribe to the suzerain-vassal theory conclude that God's omnipotence places us in a position of having no choice but to submit to Him. He sets the rules, and we obey or else.[8] Though this may seem reasonable to some, again the approach severely hinders free will. In this case there would be no real "agreement" within the relationship, at least not a heartfelt one.

A strict God-servant theology does not allow for the friendship Jesus described in John 15:15: "No longer do I call you servants, for a servant does not know what his master is doing; but I have called you friends, for all things that I heard from My Father I have made known to you." The very thought of friendship carries the idea of mutuality. Nor does God-servant theology allow for the Father-child relationship Jesus taught in John 1:12: "But as many as received Him, to them He gave the right to become children of God, to those who believe in His name."

An interesting Bible story portrays mutuality in a relationship with God as God yields to a request that is contrary to His initial command. When the prophet Ezekiel balks at God's instructions, God surprisingly changes His mind and issues a new decree (Ezek. 4). In the account God recruited Ezekiel to perform street theater "scenes" that would illustrate to Israel how He intended to respond to their rebellion. In one instance Ezekiel was commanded to bake barley cakes using human waste for fuel. This was a sign that the Israelites would themselves eat defiled bread among the Gentiles in the places where God was about to drive them. Take a look at the dialogue between God and the prophet:

> So I said, "Ah, Lord GOD! Indeed I have never defiled myself from my youth till now; I have never eaten what died of itself or was torn by beasts, nor has abominable flesh ever come into my mouth.' Then He said to me, 'See, I am giving you cow dung instead of human waste, and you shall prepare your bread over it.'"
>
> —EZEKIEL 4:14–15

This is one instance in which God changed His mind, but not in the usual way as when people repent and He then relents of His judgment. On the contrary, Ezekiel preferred something other than what God commanded, and God granted it. (This should be noted as the exception and not the rule, and I am not suggesting that we can arbitrarily question God's wisdom.)

Writing in the *International Standard Bible Encyclopedia*, George Ricker Berry says that a covenant between God and man cannot be understood as an agreement between two parties who stand on equal footing, yet there is a level of mutuality.

> To some extent...varying in different cases, it is regarded as a mutual agreement; God with His commands makes certain promises, and men agree to keep the commands, or, at any rate, the promises are conditioned on human obedience. In general, the covenant of God with men is a Divine ordinance, with signs and pledges on God's part, and with promises for human obedience and penalties for disobedience, which ordinance is accepted by men.[9]

GOD'S PLAN FOR CREATION

All relationships have ground rules. God put the world together in such a way that any violation of the principles surrounding

His creative work would damage its structure. Because of that many things are not negotiable in a relationship with God. God created a world in which He allows people to function as free agents. However, that doesn't mean He has granted us bargaining rights over how the world should operate. God has designed things to work in specific ways—all of them in agreement with His character. Some things work one way, others another way, and some things were not meant to work at all. For instance, God will not negotiate an option for a person to enter into an extramarital affair. The reason? Adultery and fornication were never meant to work. And yet some try to make them work and as a result suffer the wreckage of relationships and the loss of inner peace and joy.

On the other hand, Scripture suggests that God desires to establish an ongoing dialogue with us. From Jesus's "Come unto Me" to "Behold I stand at the door and knock," there is an unmistakable prompting to get us to make up our minds about having a relationship with Him. God's challenge to us is always, "And if it seems evil to you to serve the LORD, choose for yourselves this day whom you will serve" (Josh. 24:15). He is not demanding. He does not force our obedience.

Walking with God is a progression with ups and downs and twists and turns, mostly because exercising free will correctly is a learning process that involves getting to know God's heart. The following illustration is a crude representation of what some people believe is the way God operates:

> A woman visiting in Switzerland came to a sheepfold on one of her daily walks. Venturing in, she saw the shepherd seated on the ground with his flock around him. Nearby, on a pile of straw, lay a single sheep which seemed to be suffering. Looking closely, the woman saw that its leg was broken. Her sympathy went out to the suffering sheep and she looked up inquiringly to the shepherd, asking how it happened.
>
> "I broke it myself," said the shepherd sadly, and then explained. "Of all the sheep in my flock, this was the

most wayward. It would not obey my voice and would not follow when I was leading the flock. On more than one occasion it wandered to the edge of a perilous cliff. And not only was it disobedient itself, but it was leading other sheep astray. Based on my experience with this kind of sheep, I knew I had no choice, so I broke its leg. The next day I took food and it tried to bite me. After letting it lie alone for a couple of days, I went back and it not only took the food, but also licked my hand and showed every sign of submission and affection. And now, let me say this. When this sheep is well, it will be the model sheep of my entire flock. No sheep will hear my voice so quickly nor follow so closely. Instead of leading others away, it will be an example of devotion and obedience. In short, a complete change will come into the life of this wayward sheep. It will have learned obedience through sufferings."[10]

I sent this illustration to a number of people and received basically two kinds of responses. One group agreed with the message, but a larger second group disagreed. One particular letter was noteworthy. The man said he always had a hard time comprehending the love of God. He saw God as a frowning father figure who was perpetually disappointed with him. He felt God was always keeping score and that the bad he'd done would ultimately outweigh the good. Needless to say, that mind-set left him with incredible guilt and made it virtually impossible for him to understand and receive God's grace. He kept waiting for God to say, "OK. That's enough grace for you." This man recognized that he was serving God simply to avoid hell and that he did not truly believe he could have a joyful, loving relationship with the Father. And he realized that this is a miserable way to live.

Many people live in spiritual paralysis because they fear making a mistake, disappointing God, and possibly incurring His wrath. As the man in my previous example said, this is a miserable way to live. I've known many people who almost shipwrecked their spiritual lives by thinking that true obedience meant waiting for God to direct their every move. They felt they had no right to make a decision on their own but that God or one of His representatives must decide everything for them.

Those who teach against free will run the risk of encouraging this approach to obedience. However, the ability to choose is a key component of covenant agreement. (The other is blood, which we will discuss in the chapters ahead.) God doesn't want us to live fearful of making a move. God wants us to actively participate and cooperate with Him. That is the only way true intimacy is possible.

There is a story of a young Christian who would get up every morning, stand in front of his closet, and ask God what he should wear that day. This went on day after day until one day God spoke to him. "I'm your Father," God said, "not your mother. Get dressed." Some may chuckle at this, but I hope the point is not lost. It is not sinful to make a decision as long as it is not contrary to God's Word. (Nor is there anything wrong with seeking God for direction; the problem comes when we become paralyzed waiting for God to tell us every step we must take throughout the day because we are afraid of making mistakes.)

I remember praying about something, and in response it seemed that God was saying, "It doesn't make any difference to Me. You choose. You know My Word, and I trust you to choose correctly." What God means in a case like this is that He has set certain boundaries for operating in this life and that many personal choices can be made within those boundaries. For instance, some believe that God predestines a person's mate. However, the Scriptures indicate that we have the prerogative to choose. God sets the boundary by saying that our mate must be a Christian (2 Cor. 6:14).

Someone might ask, "Will God help us to find a mate if we ask Him to?" Absolutely! He will become involved if that is what you want. But His primary directive is, "You choose. Just make sure you choose another believer so that you are not unequally yoked together." Certainly we might ask for His approval simply so that we can be assured that we are not making a mistake. (See Genesis 24:1–28.) But we have the freedom to make wise choices within the boundaries set in Scripture. Personally I want to do everything possible to make sure that God approves of my choices. That doesn't violate my free will—that is my free will!

I want God's approval in everything. I want His perfect will. My concern is, again, for those who cannot make a single choice in life without an irrational fear of making a mistake. Hamburger or chicken tonight? You make the choice.

SUBMITTING OUR WILL TO GOD

Eternity involves some amazing responsibilities, chiefly ruling and reigning over the universe with Jesus, tasks we are being prepared for in this present life. Notice the immensity of just one of those responsibilities: "Do you not know that we shall judge angels? How much more, things that pertain to this life?" (1 Cor. 6:3).

Amazingly this task we are about to undertake will be administered through us as Christ's bride. This picture of bride and groom was, perhaps, the only way God could illustrate the unique intimacy redeemed humanity will one day have with Him, an intimacy that like marriage here on earth is possible only by some kind of mutual consent.

One of the most difficult aspects of learning to walk with God in preparation to rule with Him has to do with submission. Most of what we understand submission to mean lends itself more to the idea of dominance and suppression. In thinking about submission, sometimes God appears to be a tyrant, or at the least a King who is estranged from humanity, including Christians. The images of Him as Father, friend, and counselor often get lost in a host of other notions. When that happens, serving God takes on a negative tone.

But God is not interested in walking all over people. He is

interested in a relationship in which our will comes into alignment with His. This is something of a necessity because we cannot see things as they truly are. Submission is simply moving in the same direction God is moving. We should hardly think submission to God detestable when Jesus desired it Himself. The Bible says, "Then Jesus answered and said to them, 'Most assuredly, I say to you, the Son can do nothing of Himself, but what He sees the Father do; for whatever He does, the Son also does in like manner'" (John 5:19).

REBELLION AND THE COVENANT

Before we close this chapter, let's look briefly at how a covenant made with God deals with sin. Many believers, in wrestling with sin, see themselves as either in or out of God's kingdom based on their behavior that day. These are the same people who believe they need to get saved periodically to ensure they make it into heaven.

In later chapters we will consider how God sees and deals with sinning after conversion, but first we must understand that sinning is basically breaking God's laws. (We received a rebellious sin nature through Adam; sinning describes the wrong things we do because of that sin nature.) Technically, sinning is "missing the mark," as seen in the idea of an archer who shoots at a target and misses. But a mark must be established before it can be missed. Laws must be set in motion and understood before they can be broken. Some might say, "If a sinner is not in covenant with God, how can he break God's laws? Doesn't the covenant establish relationship and determine the stipulations of the agreement? Doesn't the covenant itself establish the target?" The Bible answers this directly:

> For the wrath of God is revealed from heaven against all ungodliness and unrighteousness of men, who suppress the truth in unrighteousness, because what may be known of God is manifest in them, for God has shown it to them. For since the creation of the world His invisible

attributes are clearly seen, being understood by the things that are made, even His eternal power and Godhead, so that they are without excuse.

—Romans 1:18–20

Without a doubt God enacted a "universal covenant" with mankind through Adam that determined the way we are to treat Him and His universe. The moment we enter this life, we enter a system of established order that we are expected to honor. The restoration and regeneration of mankind has to do with bringing humanity *back* into covenant relationship with God.

The question is, once a covenant is established with God, does a sinful act break its bond? Under the new covenant, which Jesus initiated with His death on the cross, the answer is no for the most part. The reason an act of sin doesn't negate the covenant is due to the ongoing cleansing power of Jesus's blood that is renewed through confession. As John wrote, "If we confess our sins, He is faithful and just to forgive us our sins and to cleanse us from all unrighteousness" (1 John 1:9).

This, of course, is not a license to sin but is God's wonderful grace extended to those who continue to remain humble in their relationship with Him. The bond of the new covenant ceases to exist only when a person consciously walks away from the relationship by *practicing* sin with the attitude that they no longer want God in their lives. While we occasionally fall into sin, that does not break our covenant with God, though it does diminish the blessing, joy, authority, power, and closeness that come with a personal relationship with God.

CHAPTER 5

Sealed in Blood

And it came to pass, when the sun went down and it was dark, that behold, there appeared a smoking oven and a burning torch that passed between those pieces. On the same day the LORD made a covenant with Abram, saying: "To your descendants I have given this land, from the river of Egypt to the great river, the River Euphrates."

—GENESIS 15:17–18

FEW THINGS ARE as emotionally draining as the anguish resulting from a failed agreement. Somebody promised to do something but didn't follow through. There was a written contract, but it made no difference to one of the parties. A pledge of fidelity got tossed aside during a moment of selfishness.

I sold a man some things he agreed to pay me for later. To this day I have not seen the money. I've tried to reach him by phone and by letter, but he has avoided me. There's not much I can do about it. The issue both frustrates and angers me. I'm frustrated because I have little recourse. I'm angered because I thought the guy could be trusted.

It seems reasonable to expect people to keep their word. When they don't, it's easy to become disheartened and upset. Most of us have been disappointed by someone who failed to keep their part of a bargain. That's why, whenever possible, it is important to get a guarantee.

Just as in agreements between individuals, covenants with God involve two parties who are each expected to fulfill their end of the bargain. Most would agree that God can be trusted to keep His Word; it's reasonable to think His promise is as good as He is. Unfortunately the same is not true of us. Although our promise may be as good as we are, we are not very good. The sad fact is that our fallen nature makes our word unreliable. The apostle Paul said it well: "For what I am doing, I do not understand. For what I will to do, that I do not practice; but what I hate, that I do" (Rom. 7:15). The spirit is willing, and we want to do the right thing, but the flesh is weak (Matt. 26:41), and for whatever reason we don't always do what is correct.

So what can mere humans offer an eternal God to assure Him that we will uphold our part of the covenant relationship? Our "life," it turns out, is the only guarantee that is powerful enough to satisfy God. So then if a person wants to enter into covenant with God, he must guarantee it with his life.

Although the idea of entering into covenant with God is a basic tenet of Christian theology, the concept isn't often explored; therefore many are unfamiliar with what the Scriptures say on the subject. In order to effect a permanent bond with humanity, God established relational covenants and required that they be signed in blood. That means the agreement must be guaranteed by blood. If for some reason the covenant is broken, the only payment that will suffice is the person's life, for "almost all things are purified with blood, and without shedding of blood is no remission" (Heb. 9:22).

Every agreement God makes with us is guaranteed by blood and in this way God laid the groundwork for His plan to redeem humanity. The two Hebrew words *karat* and *brith*, which together mean "to cut a covenant," represent this important biblical concept. Though other kinds of covenants have been forged throughout history (salt treaties, for instance), blood covenants have been used universally to establish lasting relationships.

Blood covenants do two important things. First, they unite two parties into a solid union. As nineteenth-century clergyman H. Clay Trumbull explains, "The inter-commingling of the blood of two organisms is…equivalent to the inter-commingling of the lives, of the personalities, of the natures, thus brought together; so that there is, thereby and thenceforward, one life in the two bodies, a common life between two friends."[1]

Second, blood covenants establish blood as the price to be paid should the agreement be broken. It is the guarantee that the agreed upon stipulations will not be disregarded. God does not take broken covenants lightly. We read in the Book of Ezekiel: "'Since he despised the oath by breaking the covenant, and in fact gave his hand and still did all these things, he shall not escape.' Therefore thus says the Lord God: 'As I live, surely My oath which he despised, and My covenant which he broke, I will recompense on his own head'" (Ezek. 17:18–19). The penalty for breaking a covenant with God is indeed stiff.

I realize that you may have never heard God's covenant with us put in these terms. This explanation may even sound a little bizarre. But I guarantee that by understanding covenant in this way, you will better understand what redemption really means and how God manifested His love for us through Jesus and freed us from guilt, condemnation, and hopelessness.

MADE AND PAID

As I previously stated, a blood covenant is "made" in blood and if broken must be paid for in blood.[2] As elementary as it may sound, this "made and paid" arrangement has been the basis of covenant-making not only in the Bible but also in many cultures of the world for thousands of years. Throughout the ages "blood covenanting" has symbolized the coming together of separate lives into a single identity. In its purest sense a blood covenant gives meaning and purpose to a relationship. It secures the union of personality and character. The life of one vitalizes the life of the other and places each at the disposal of the other.[3]

Historically there seems to have been a universal understanding that lasting agreements were somehow established with blood. Trumbull writes that people groups all over the world believed there was an "absolute oneness of nature through a oneness of blood."[4]

David Livingstone, a missionary and explorer to Africa in the late 1800s, described many African cultures securing agreements on the basis of blood. In his *Missionary Travels and Researches in South Africa* he wrote about a blood covenant rite called *Kasendi* held between his traveling companion, Pitsane, and Sambanza, the husband of a female chief. Livingstone describes the "cutting" of the covenant this way:

> The hands of the parties are joined (in this case Pitsane and Sambanza were the parties engaged); small incisions are made on the clasped hands, on the pits of the stomach of each, and on the right cheeks and foreheads. A small quantity of blood is taken off from these points in both parties by means of a stalk of grass. The blood from one person is put into a pot of beer, and that of the second into another; each then drinks the other's blood, and they are supposed to become perpetual friends or relations. During the drinking of the beer, some of the party continue beating the ground with short clubs, and utter sentences by way of ratifying the treaty. The men belonging to each then finish the beer. The principals in the performance of "Kasendi" are henceforth considered blood-relations, and are bound to disclose to each other any impending evil. If Sekeletu should resolve to attack the Balonda, Pitsane would be under obligation to give Sambanza warning to escape, and so on the other side.[5]

At one point Livingstone accidentally became a blood relation to a young woman when he operated on a tumor on her forearm. The blood from the incision squirted into Livingstone's eye, and as he was wiping it away, the woman said, "You were a friend before, now you are a blood-relation; and when you pass this way, always send me word, that I may cook food for you."[6]

Journalist Henry Morton Stanley, also an explorer in Africa, reported having his flesh cut many times in making covenants with the people of that land. The method for sealing these agreements in blood was quite simple. Typically a small cut was made in the forearm of each participant and the blood was mingled by rubbing the arms together. Other methods for sealing blood covenants have existed, but cutting the flesh in this manner was common.[7]

In many cultures blood covenants were accompanied by lavish ceremonies, including the exchange of gifts, a feast, and a memorial of some kind. The feast created an atmosphere of celebration. A memorial then was established to remind both parties and their descendants of the agreement. Historically memorials have been marked by large piles of rocks (Deut. 27:2–8; Josh. 4:1–7) or the planting of trees (Gen. 21:33).

In many cases families and others under the authority of the original covenant-makers were also expected to abide by the terms of the agreement. Some were even required to personally ratify the agreement with their own blood, as was the case with circumcision initiated through God's covenant with Abraham.

The idea is that this blood would forge a lasting pact between them and that their friendship would continue for the rest of their lives. H. Clay Trumbull writes that though blood covenanting has been practiced in every corner of the globe, "it has been strangely overlooked by biblical critics and biblical commentators generally, in these later centuries."[8]

THE PRICE OF A FAILED AGREEMENT

The significance of blood in establishing covenants with God is often misunderstood in Christian circles. Most believers recognize the importance of blood to cleanse from sin, but few understand the need for blood in making the initial agreement. Blood is literally what puts the agreement into effect. For instance, it is commonly thought that the New Testament covenant was sealed on the cross, but that is not so. The blood Jesus shed on the cross was actually the payment for a failed agreement. Agreements must be in force before they can be broken. Wycliffe Bible Translators missionary Don Richardson witnessed a powerful example of blood covenant while working in Papua New Guinea. One day Don observed a treaty exchange between two tribes that had been at war. The chief of one tribe lifted his baby son high in the air and then presented him to the chief of the warring tribe. It was explained to Don that this baby would be raised by the other tribe. If the child was ever harmed, the agreement would be broken and the offended tribe would seek the blood of the other.

The baby was the "peace child." His life sealed the agreement. Blood, in the form of this living child, ratified the agreement, and blood would be required if the agreement was broken. This was the break that Don needed to present the gospel message in a way the people could understand. He was able to explain the agreement God made with all people by providing His own peace child, Jesus Christ. Our peace with God was secured through Jesus in what we call the new agreement—the new covenant. But knowing we would fail to honor the agreement, God took it a step further and paid the price for our failure by sacrificing the life of His own Son.[9]

Because God requires blood to "make agreements" and to "pay" for failed agreements, some people may perceive Him as a bloodthirsty deity looking to wreak havoc on humanity. He is nothing of the kind. He is the almighty God who seeks a lasting relationship with humanity, one so significant and perpetual that it must be sealed in blood.

God is in need of nothing. He is complete within Himself but desires to be in fellowship with humanity. He wants to be close to us, and it pleases Him when we come to Him through Jesus Christ. The blood is a sign of how sacred and binding God intends our relationship with Him to be. He is not looking to destroy humanity; to the contrary, He wants to have an intimate union with us that lasts forever.

CHAPTER 6

The Old Testament Blood Covenant

Therefore not even the first covenant
was dedicated without blood.

—Hebrews 9:18

G OD ESTABLISHED THE old covenant to help us understand the nature of all eternal agreements made with Him. In this chapter we will look at the history of God's covenants with mankind to get a better understanding of the new covenant established through Christ.

There has always been a covenant between God and man. The first was what some call the Edenic covenant. It allowed man to enter the Garden of Eden, and it was universal in that it established how mankind was to relate to God and the universe and how He would relate to us. All of Adam's descendants were under this covenant, and this is the covenant Adam broke when he sinned. This is believed to have been a blood covenant because God sacrificed animals to create skins to cover Adam and Eve after they sinned, in keeping with the "made and paid" principle discussed in chapter 5.

Later God established the old covenant, or old agreement, between Himself and the children of Israel. Many people think Abraham was the one through whom God established His covenant with Israel, because Abraham was the father of the Israelites. But it was actually during Moses's leadership that God established and ratified the accord. This agreement was a blood covenant that was "signed" (validated) through circumcision, which became the "sign" of the agreement. (We will look more closely at the "sign" and "signature" in chapters 8 and 9.) Covenants were made before the time of Moses, but none is ever referred to as the "old" covenant that would ultimately be replaced by the "new" after it had served its purpose (Rom. 8:4; 13:8; Gal. 5:14; Eph. 2:15).

The old agreement (covenant), sometimes called the Mosaic covenant, was intended to run its course after it completed its purpose, which was to show us that we couldn't make ourselves right by successfully living up to its standards. It was always intended to be replaced when Jesus established the new agreement (new covenant). Malachi prophesied that this would occur: "'Behold, I send My messenger, and he will prepare the way before Me. And the Lord, whom you seek, will suddenly come to His temple, even *the Messenger of the covenant*, in whom you delight. Behold, He is coming,' says the LORD of hosts" (Mal. 3:1, emphasis added).

The prophecy was confirmed in the New Testament after Jesus's death. "But now He has obtained a more excellent ministry, inasmuch as He is also Mediator of a better covenant, which was established on better promises" (Heb. 8:6). Each step between the old agreement and the new was part of a divine plan that would enable God and mankind to unite in fellowship forever.

The real difference between the two covenants is clarified by Paul in his writings to the Romans: "For what the law could not do in that it was weak through the flesh, God did by sending His own Son in the likeness of sinful flesh, on account of sin: He condemned sin in the flesh, that the righteous requirement of the law might be fulfilled in us who do not walk according to the flesh but according to the Spirit" (Rom. 8:3–4).

Paul acknowledged that the law was good in that it tells us what righteousness really is, but it gave no help in making us righteous. The good news, then, was that God by His Spirit would help us become righteous if we would simply accept the offer. It is as if God said, "I will come to help you become righteous if you will allow Me to live very close to you, closer than any earthly relationship." The whole idea amounted to God's Spirit strengthening us to stand against sin. But this could only happen by way of a covenant agreement "signed" by Jesus.

Adam lost real fellowship with God after he sinned in the Garden of Eden. Before that Adam enjoyed a close connection with God, filled with love and faith, as well as holiness and righteousness that were a natural result of their fellowship. It is still the same today. God wants closeness based on faith rather than human effort to live righteously.

This is why "works," used to refer to personal attempts to perform righteous acts, is discounted in the Scriptures as a way to salvation. God says, "No matter how hard you try to be good without Me in your life, it will never work." A religious life without Jesus is useless. No matter how good you try to be or how much you think you have accomplished, you will always fall short. It is like trying to fix a computer without knowing how it works, or trying to please the boss without knowing what he wants. Only by getting close to Jesus through His indwelling Holy Spirit are we able to do what is right.

A MODEL FOR FUTURE COVENANTS

As mentioned previously, the old covenant is different from the one God made with Abraham. But it is important to understand the Abrahamic covenant because it helps illustrate how God puts covenants together. Many Christians live frustrated lives because they don't know how to relate to God. The relationship God established with Abraham is a model for how all relationships with Him are to be established.

As with all blood covenants God's agreement with Abraham—commonly called the Abrahamic covenant—was to be signed in blood, and it was to be "everlasting." God promised that through this covenant He would bless and protect Abraham's descendants *forever*. (We will explore the ongoing benefits of the Abrahamic covenant in chapter 27.)

When God established His covenant with Abraham, it too was a blood covenant. But God is Spirit, so it would have been impossible for Him to cut His forearm and mix His blood with Abraham's. In Genesis 15:9–17 God used the blood of a heifer, a goat, and a ram to make the agreement. He used *substitutionary* blood, a concept that will become exceedingly important when we look at Christ's sacrifice.

In Genesis 15 God instructed Abraham to cut the animals in two down the middle and place each piece opposite the other. God then passed between the bloody animal halves like "a smoking oven and a burning torch" (v. 17). God's passing through the pieces of flesh was His way of placing His signature on the agreement. It was God's way of acknowledging the blood in covenant relationship. But this was only the beginning of His blood covenant with Abraham.[1]

Later Abraham would be required to ratify the agreement himself. Ratification would require the use of his own blood— the blood of circumcision, which was to be the "sign" of the covenant and the signature that sealed the accord. Genesis 15:18 says, "On the same day the LORD made [Hebrew *karat*, "to cut"] a covenant with Abram." (Abram was Abraham's name before God changed it.) Then in Genesis 17:10–11 Abraham's flesh was cut by circumcision in order to complete the agreement. God said, "This is My covenant which you shall keep, between Me and you and your descendants after you: Every male child among you shall be circumcised; and you shall be circumcised in the flesh of your foreskins, and it shall be a sign of the covenant between you and Me."[2]

Blood was required on both God's part and man's part to ratify the agreement. In Abraham's case circumcision served both as a way to "make" the agreement with God and as the "signature" upon it. (Typically we think of signatures as something written by hand, but any distinctive mark attributed to a person can be regarded as a signature—an X, for instance; blood has long been an acceptable mark for signing an agreement.)

This distinction between "making" and "signing" a covenant may sound trivial, but it is actually quite important. Blood covenants with God are not all "made" through circumcision, but eventually they all must be "signed" through circumcision.

Scripture mentions three ways covenant agreements have been made: blood on the doorposts (Exod. 12:7–8), passing between the bloody halves of animals (Jer. 34:18), and the sprinkling of the blood of animals (Exod. 24:8). Yet even when these methods were used, God still required the signature of circumcision. I stress this point because even today under the new covenant God requires the signature of circumcision— circumcision of the heart. That was always His goal; the agreements made before Christ were pointing toward this plan for the new covenant.

The seriousness of making a covenant in blood and then failing to keep it is spelled out in Jeremiah 34:18–20, where the prophet pronounces God's judgment on the offenders: "And I will give the men who have transgressed My covenant, who have not performed the words of the covenant which they made before Me, when they cut the calf in two and passed between the parts of it...I will give them into the hand of their enemies and into the hand of those who seek their life. Their dead bodies shall be for meat for the birds of the heaven and the beasts of the earth."[3] Again we see that a covenant made in blood must be paid for in blood if broken.

At this point it may seem extremely difficult to unite with God, but stay with me. We will soon see how God's grace allows for the joyous fulfillment of all His desires and commands.

CHAPTER 7

The Rules of the Agreement

This is My covenant which you shall keep, between
Me and you and your descendants after you: Every
male child among you shall be circumcised.

—GENESIS 17:10

EVERY AGREEMENT STIPULATES certain terms, commit-ments, and responsibilities accepted by both parties. These stipulations say, "I will do such and such if you will do thus and so." If the parties involved are able to exercise free will in the process of putting an agreement together, we say that the agreement is mutual (i.e., shared and reciprocated). Most covenants are in some way mutual, as each party expects some give and take. If there is no element of consensus, it probably isn't a true agreement and therefore cannot be called a covenant.

The real idea behind agreement is heartfelt consent. People may give assent to a dictator, but it is usually under duress. The policies of one are forced upon the other. This violates the true essence of covenant. Love, admiration, and respect are impossible in an atmosphere of rigid control, and it is not really an agreement because one party never really agreed.

In the case of covenants with God it's hard to imagine that He would want to force allegiance on the people He desires in His company. This is especially clear when we read of the Father's heart in the parable of the prodigal son (Luke 15:11–32) and the concern of the shepherd in the case of the lost sheep (Luke 15:4–10). These stories point to a person interested in far more than just telling people what to do and how to live. And they confirm the old saying that "rules without relationship end in rebellion."

If God wanted to relate by force, He could do that easily. One word from His lips and all humanity would lie prostrate before Him. It is clear that He does not desire this kind of blind obedience, yet we cannot deny that rules in a relationship with God must, in fact, exist and that we will need to take a careful look at them.

Again there are some who believe covenants with God are all unilateral, meaning that mankind has no say except to consent by threat of hell to the covenant. To some that is the only thing that makes sense considering the fact that God is omnipotent. That fact, however, doesn't necessarily mean covenants with Him lack mutuality. The possibility that one party is more influential or powerful than the other does not diminish the importance of reaching an agreement.

Covenants with God are not one-sided. If they were, we would at best be His servants with no hope of becoming His friends. And yet Jesus told His disciples shortly before His death, "No longer do I call you servants, for a servant does not know what his master is doing; but I have called you friends, for all things that I heard from My Father I have made known to you" (John 15:15).

Having said that, let me make this point clear: the rules of the universe, including the rules that govern relationships, are unilateral. They have to be, simply because sin has caused every man to do what is right in his own eyes (Deut. 12:8). God's standards are not negotiable. They exist because they are right in relation to the creation. But covenanting with God is not just about rules—it is about "relationship."

A closer look at God's standards, or rules, reveals not prohibition as much as protection. For instance, the commandment to not commit adultery is really a bid to protect marriage. The commandment to not steal is really God's desire to protect personal property. The commandment to not lie is meant to protect truth. I can buy into this as a reasonable requirement in order to live in God's world. I simply can't live this out without God's help in Jesus. That again was why we needed the new covenant.

FORCED OBEDIENCE RUINS RELATIONSHIPS

The tone of Scripture indicates that God in His mercy and love is not interested in coercing us to do His will. Anything He requires of us is for our own good.

As my friend Rick Kline explained, God did not create us and decide to only love and bless us if we chose to obey Him. God didn't place having a loving relationship with us secondary to having us obey Him. I like the way Rick makes this point:

> If we have the idea that we have to earn God's blessings, doesn't this imply that we receive His love out of merit, that a loving relationship with God is possible by good works? We could not live long enough to do enough to earn God's loving grace. God's grace has always preceded obedience to law. For example, in Exodus 3:5 God told Moses to take off his shoes because he was standing on holy ground. Notice that Moses was already on holy ground. He did not have to qualify to be on holy ground by taking off his shoes first. It was grace that allowed Moses to be there initially. Later, God delivered Israel from Egypt and then gave the Law (*Torah*). Notice that the Law came after God's grace in delivering Israel. They did not have to qualify for deliverance. Certainly, we must live a clean life. But a fisherman cleans the fish after they are caught, not before.[1]

While rejoicing over God's grace and His willingness to forgive sin, one may fail to realize that the earthly consequences of sin can leave emotional and physical scars—even death. Sin not only creates its own penalty; it also executes its own judgment.

The disease AIDS is a good example. Here is an illness often contracted through activities the Bible condemns, namely fornication, adultery, homosexuality, and illicit drug use. Unfortunately innocent victims, especially children, are often caught in the web of another's sin. The virus can be passed to a newborn from an infected mother, who may have contracted it from an unfaithful husband. God's rules are there to protect us and others from the spiral of pain sin leaves in its wake.

In a similar way, when God covenanted with Abraham, He wanted the relationship to benefit more than just Abraham. Of course, Abraham was important to God, but God's plan would ultimately impact all of humanity forever; the blessings would not be only Abraham's. God selected Abraham and his descendants to be the people through whom the Savior and Messiah would come. Having a covenant people was His plan A, and if Abraham had been unwilling to respond, God would not have come up with a plan B; He would have found someone else. God knew that He would find someone who would agree to the stipulations of the covenant, thereby allowing Him to fulfill His divine plan.

GOD REACHES OUT TO US

God reaches out to people. Sin within the human heart prevents humanity from reaching out to Him. The Bible tells us, "'There is none righteous, no, not one; there is none who understands; *there is none who seeks after God*. They have all turned aside; they have together become unprofitable; there is none who does good, no, not one'" (Rom. 3:10–12, emphasis added).

For emphasis, let me go back to a previous thought. The lord-servant or suzerain-vassal treaties, commonly called "suzerainty treaties," acknowledge differing levels of authority and responsibility between the parties involved in the agreement. Within its basic structure the lord, suzerain, or king simply made known the stipulations of the contract, and the vassal or servant either agreed to or declined the contract. And again, this procedure was characteristic of many ancient cultures for thousands of years.

Interestingly the Jewish people do not hold the view that God only wants to dominate mankind; instead they see Him as wanting an ongoing relational intimacy with us. Noted author Rabbi Harold Kushner explains:

> The immense importance of seeing the revelation of Sinai as the forming of a Covenant, and the Torah as the record of that Covenant, is that it proclaims the idea that God and Man have obligations to each other. We owe God something, the obligation to discern and choose the good, in exchange for His giving us life, health, food to eat, and people to love us....And the idea of Covenant articulates the idea that we can expect things from God, that He will not be an arbitrary ruler.[2]

Although Kushner's statement could be viewed as "good deeds" theology, it still reflects a Jewish understanding that God desires a personal relationship with us based on some form of mutual covenant.

On the surface some of God's dealings with people (especially in the Old Testament) may seem to suggest that God is a taskmaster who keeps a constant eye on humankind to enforce obedience. Judging only from God's statements before and after the fall—"you shall not eat of the tree" and then "cursed is the ground"—it does sound as if He is only interested in telling people what to do.

A closer examination, however, reveals something far different. God visited the garden to fellowship with Adam as a friend to a friend. (In fact, the entire biblical teaching on the reconciliation of mankind to God through Christ suggests people coming back into "fellowship" with their Creator. The Greek word for "reconciliation," *katallage*, means, "atonement," or becoming "at one," creating a picture of harmony, bond, and agreement.)

After Adam sinned, God wanted to prevent him from self-destructing. Yes, God warned him sternly about things that would harm him, but God was not speaking as an oppressive overlord but as a concerned Father.

Some sectors of the religious world shun the idea of a personal God, but if God is not personal, we have no hope of fellowshipping with Him. Over three hundred years ago a monk named Brother Lawrence discovered that he could enter into God's presence moment by moment throughout the day no matter where he was or what he was doing. His book *The Practice of the Presence of God*, which stands as one of the great pieces of Christian literature, persuasively presents the opportunity available to all of us to get to know God on a personal level. I highly recommend it.

COMMAND VS. DEMAND

In Genesis 1:28 God told Adam to replenish the earth.[3] Some see this as God's first command to mankind. But what exactly is meant by the word *command*? Is it the same thing as a demand? For some *command* connotes a harshness, much like the word *demand*. Certainly the word *command* seems out of sync with the idea of an agreement. Perhaps part of the problem lies in differentiating between a command and a demand. The word *command* can be a stated condition that is expected within an existing relationship or conditional agreement, while a *demand* suggests the threat of forced obedience one might expect in an unconditional agreement.

Yet regardless of command or demand, if a person doesn't accept Jesus, he goes to hell. In this regard what difference does it make how we view God's attitude in what He says? First of all I must reiterate that we do have choices, two of them: 1) to stay where we are in the kingdom of death and darkness, or 2) to change kingdoms. This is a rescue mission, not a threat to obey or else. God is saying to us, "I'm not a demanding God. The one you currently serve (Satan) operates that way. I'm simply saying that if you come to Me, you must realize that My kingdom, which is for you and not against you, is made in certain ways. And since that new kingdom is right now, you need to know how it functions. I'm simply telling you how things work."

To fully convey God's desire for a friend (Abraham), deep fellowship (Enoch), and divine favor (Noah), the cultural definition of the word *commandment* has to be retooled and the word *demand* put on the shelf. Jesus gives the impression that God wants to fellowship with us as a father desires a close relationship with his children. In telling our children what to do, is it not our intent to guide them in a relational manner that yields a closeness that lasts long after they are grown?

Some suggest that God's terms for establishing and maintaining a relationship with Him are spelled out in the Ten Commandments. In reality there were more than just ten commandments given as mandates for sustaining the old agreement.[4] There were additional commands called ordinances that existed in the time of Moses. Anyone who wanted a relationship with God needed not only to *know* all of them but also to *obey* all of them. That's a frightening thought. The human spirit can be overwhelmed with hopelessness when faced with an endless list of things to do.

TWO STIPULATIONS

Jesus severely slashed this burdensome to-do list by showing that there are really only two stipulations in any agreement made with God: to love (respect) Him and to love (respect) others. Literally all of the other commandments and ordinances hinge on these two basic requirements (Matt. 22:36–40). Why then were there so many commandments in Old Testament times? The hardness of the human heart made it necessary for God to spell everything out in detail. Examine the many commandments of Scripture, and you'll see that all of them either explain or amplify those fundamental two—to love God and to love others. In reality all of the commands of God are relational, as they are based on the way we treat Him and others.

In return for honoring God and others, God agrees to uphold basically two provisions: 1) to bless us (Gen. 12:3; 17:6) and 2) to protect us from our enemies, especially the enemy of our souls (Gen. 17:8). Where Satan and his demons have held humanity captive, God stands as a shield of protection once the covenant is in place:

> Then your light shall break forth like the morning, your healing shall spring forth speedily, and your righteousness shall go before you; the glory of the Lord shall be your rear guard.
>
> —Isaiah 58:8

> No weapon formed against you shall prosper.
>
> —Isaiah 54:17

> He [the Father] has delivered us from the power of darkness and conveyed us into the kingdom of the Son of His love.
>
> —Colossians 1:13

How about that? God promises to guard people who are in covenant with Him. Jewish scholars believe this promise is still in effect today. Again Rabbi Harold Kushner explains, "God invites the entire Israelite people to join with Him in a Covenant, a contract. The Israelites promise to live a distinctive, moral, God-centered life, and God for His part promises to bless the people with His presence, give them a homeland of their own, and protect them there."[5]

CHAPTER 8

The "Sign" of the Agreement

*And you shall be circumcised in the flesh of your foreskins,
and it shall be a sign of the covenant between Me and you.*

—Genesis 17:11

A SIGNATURE IS AN important aspect of almost all agreements. It confirms a person's willingness to honor the stipulations set forth in the contract. It is something that can be pointed to later as an indication that the party did, in fact, agree to the terms of the agreement. Today most signatures are made with pen and paper, but this is a relatively new development. Not too long ago a handshake or a person's word was sufficient to establish an agreement; they were his bond.

Before any of these means were used, agreements usually were sealed with blood. A person's own blood, sometimes shared from a cut in the forearm, stood as a guarantee that the agreement would never be broken. It was the "signature" on the agreement. There was also a "sign" of agreements made with God, and that was circumcision, as we see in the covenant between God and Abraham: "And you shall be circumcised in the flesh of your foreskins, and it shall be a sign of the covenant between Me and you" (Gen. 17:11).

Notice the words "sign of the covenant."[1] Circumcision was the physical evidence of a covenant made in blood. And the sign of circumcision was not something just between God and Abraham; it was for all humanity. This is clear from Genesis 17:10: "This is My covenant which you shall keep, *between Me and you and your descendants after you*: Every male child among you shall be circumcised" (emphasis added). So we find both "signature" and "sign" in covenant making. One, the signature, is made with blood when entering into the agreement. The other, the sign, is the witness that the covenant has indeed been established.

WITNESSES TO AN AGREEMENT

Today many agreements need to be notarized. This usually involves a formal witnessing process that helps establish the authenticity of a contract. If the legitimacy of the contract is questioned, the witness or witnesses may help resolve the issue. Their signatures not only confirm the conditions of the contract but also attest to the fact that a contract was made in the first place.

Circumcision was highly important to a Jew as it served as a witness to an agreement with God. Everyone in Israel recognized that a circumcised person had a relationship with God; that may have been a corporate identity more than an individual one, but it was important nonetheless. A male child was to be circumcised at eight days old (Lev. 12:3). Circumcision represented Israel's corporate allegiance to God.[2] This act of corporate obedience made Israel's culture different from that of the surrounding nations. Today Israel is still infused with a strong sense of community and nationalism that was originally instilled through covenanting with God.

The church also was intended to function in a corporate manner. That is why it is often referred to as a body. Salvation is a personal matter based on an agreement with God that requires a personal signature. In other words, a person must exercise his or her own free will in order to have a covenant relationship with God. Being born into a Christian home, going to church, or even practicing the Christian faith doesn't establish a covenant bond with God. In fact, a person can be baptized in water and circumcised in the flesh and still not know God.[3] This is why Paul stated that from a purely physical standpoint, circumcision is worthless for salvation (1 Cor. 7:19).

The physical mark of circumcision was symbolic of God's true desire for humanity—heart circumcision. Scripture points toward this plan even in the Old Testament: "And the LORD your God will circumcise your heart and the heart of your descendants, to love the LORD your God with all your heart and with all your soul, that you may live" (Deut. 30:6). And, "Circumcise yourselves to the LORD, and take away the foreskins of your hearts, you men of Judah and inhabitants of Jerusalem, lest My fury come forth like fire, and burn so that no one can quench it, because of the evil of your doings" (Jer. 4:4).

You don't have to be around a true Christian very long before you realize that he or she is "marked." This "circumcision of the heart" sets people apart from the world in their motives, goals, character, and speech. They are different because something profound has occurred within them. They don't have to try to be different—they just are.

Bobby was a rough and tough gang member. When Bobby met Jesus, his life was completely transformed. He didn't become weak, but he did become tender before God. When we met, there was an almost instant rapport. We talked about the things of the Lord as if we were brothers who had known each other for a long time. Bobby is now a marked man—marked by his Lord Jesus Christ and by heart circumcision. You can sense it by his tenderness and humility within the strong and bold character he is developing in Jesus.

REFUSING THE "SIGN"

In Israel during Moses's era a person could not remain an integral part of the community without submitting to a covenant relationship with God through circumcision. A person unwilling to acknowledge God through circumcision was forced to live outside the camp. It might seem harsh that God would require individuals to separate themselves from the community because they refused to sign a covenant with Him. But

God was making it clear that there were two kingdoms on earth, one controlled by Him and the other by Satan.

If a person wanted to rebel against God, he could choose to do so. But he could not continue in rebellion and live in close fellowship with those who were in covenant relationship with God. They were to be separated, as Genesis 17:14 says, "And the uncircumcised male child, who is not circumcised in the flesh of his foreskin, that person shall be cut off from his people; he has broken My covenant." Later Jesus affirmed the principle of separation when He said, "He who is not with Me is against Me, and he who does not gather with Me scatters abroad" (Matt. 12:30).

The principle of ex-communication is still in effect today. The new covenant calls us to separate from those who practice a sinful lifestyle. Paul addressed those within the church who have "a form of godliness but [deny] its power," and he said, "From such people turn away" (2 Tim. 3:5; see also 1 Cor. 5:1–5). This does not mean that in the normal daily practices of life that we have nothing to do with nonbelievers. Again, the apostle Paul said, "I wrote to you in my epistle not to keep company with sexually immoral people. Yet I certainly did not mean with the sexually immoral people of this world, or with the covetous, or extortionists, or idolaters, since then you would need to go out of the world" (1 Cor. 5:9–10). (We will discuss this further in chapter 10.) No, we cannot remove ourselves from the world, but Scripture tells us we should not have close fellowship with a believer who is living in sin.

CHAPTER 9

Circumcision of the Flesh

He who is born in your house and he who is bought
with your money must be circumcised, and My covenant
shall be in your flesh for an everlasting covenant.

—Genesis 17:13

CIRCUMCISION IN ITS natural form is the removal of the foreskin of male or female genitalia. The practice is most commonly performed on males, but in some cultures women are also circumcised, usually in order to reduce sexual desire. Although the position of this book is that God is the originator of the idea of circumcision for covenant-making purposes, there is little historical data on the subject of circumcision itself. It is practiced in a number of cultures today throughout America, Africa, New Guinea, Australia, and the Pacific Islands. However, it is not found widely in South America or Europe, except among the Jewish communities there.

Circumcision is still practiced among followers of Judaism and Islam, but not among the Hindu, Buddhist, and Confucian societies. The Christian church, for the most part, has no specific doctrine on the subject, though many Christian males are circumcised, no doubt as a result of the Jewish influence on Christianity. An estimated 85 percent of American males are circumcised. Beyond religious conviction the argument for circumcision is based on health concerns. Though controversial the thought is that circumcision helps to prevent certain diseases that occur between the penile layers of the skin. Opponents of the idea suggest that any increase in disease among the uncircumcised is the result of poor hygiene.[1]

There is a strong possibility that circumcision goes all the way back to the beginning of creation. The skins used to cover Adam and Eve and the sacrifices in Noah's time (Gen. 8:20–22) indicate that a blood covenant was in effect. If circumcision is a normal part of covenant-making with God, then this practice likely existed long before the time of Abraham. Ancient Egyptian art predating Abraham depicts the custom.

MORE THAN CUTTING FLESH

In the Old Testament circumcision was more than an operation. Certainly it was a daily reminder of the Israelites' agreement with God, but it also symbolized humility before God. Circumcision was a natural picture of a spiritual commitment. We read in Leviticus, "If their uncircumcised hearts are humbled, and they accept their guilt—then I will remember My covenant" (Lev. 26:41–42; see also Gen. 9:15).

Circumcision was also a reminder that the sinful works of the flesh had to be destroyed in order to produce spiritual life. Whatever else it may have symbolized, circumcision was a requirement for entering into a relationship with God. Author G. E. Farley points out that, "unfortunately, as noted by Jeremiah 4:4 and in Deuteronomy 10:16; 30:6, many of the natural Jews were circumcised physically, but failed to realize the symbolic and spiritual significance of the act."[2]

The Hebrew people became widely known for their practice of circumcision. The physical procedure was eventually associated with both the idea of spiritual purity and national pride. Nations such as the Philistines, who were outside of covenant relationship with God, were referred to as the "uncircumcised" (1 Sam. 17:36).

Today circumcision is still widely practiced among Jews. Rabbi Harold Kushner writes that circumcision "identifies the Jewish child as a member of the Covenant with God by virtue of his birth as a Jew into a Jewish family."[3] How different this is from Christianity, where a covenant with God is established only through a personal relationship with God through Jesus for each individual.

WOMEN AND CIRCUMCISION

If "personal" circumcision was necessary for establishing a relationship with God, then obviously we have a problem with women entering into covenant with Him on this basis. In Moses's day God apparently allowed a woman to ratify the agreement through her obedience in permitting the male children of her household to be circumcised. In Exodus 4:24–26 Moses was in the process of entering into a covenant with God through circumcision. In studying this passage I believe his wife, Zipporah, balked at the idea and refused to allow her sons to be circumcised. Because of her reluctance, God confronted Moses and demanded that all who were under His blessing and protection sign the covenant agreement through circumcision.

Here was a situation where people were living under covenant blessing and protection without having signed the agreement. No one was forcing them to sign. At the same time they could not live with those who had signed the agreement. If they didn't want a relationship with God, they could leave and go elsewhere.[4] God will not allow a person to live under the covenant blessings and protections of another. Each person must enter into the agreement by way of choice.

Later in Exodus 12:43–48 God disallowed foreigners from observing covenant rights in an ordinance called Passover without first being circumcised. But in reality if a person didn't make an agreement with God and sign it through circumcision, he remained at enmity with Him and continued to reside in the kingdom of darkness (1 John 5:19). At issue was the need to become a part of God's household. Those of other nations were allowed to join the people of Israel and participate in their covenant relationship with God only if they agreed to be circumcised.

CIRCUMCISION IN THE NEW TESTAMENT

Is circumcision still required today in order to enter into covenant relationship with God? The whole point of circumcision can be summed up in Deuteronomy 10:16: "Therefore circumcise the foreskin of your heart, and be stiff-necked no longer."

This verse foreshadows a similar teaching in Romans 2:28–29: "For he is not a Jew who is one outwardly, nor is circumcision that which is outward in the flesh; but he is a Jew who is one inwardly; and circumcision is that of the heart, in the Spirit, not in the letter; whose praise is not from men but from God."

God restores us to Himself by changing the heart through spiritual circumcision. Our defiled condition makes it impossible to commune with Him until that change takes place. Our present condition cannot withstand His presence. We would no doubt die if our fallen nature were to be exposed, even momentarily, to God's overwhelming glory. Any restoration to God must begin with inward change. This happens when a sinner hears the gospel and allows the Holy Spirit to enter his heart. That may sound simplistic, but something amazing happens inside a person when heart circumcision occurs as God's Spirit takes up residence within the human spirit, fulfilling the words, "Therefore, if anyone is in Christ, he is a new creation" (2 Cor. 5:17).

Heart circumcision can also be described as the process of developing a humble and contrite spirit (which begins with a repentant attitude). As the heart yields to God through Jesus, He literally enters into that person. "For thus says the High and Lofty One who inhabits eternity, whose name is Holy: 'I dwell in the high and holy place, with him who has a contrite and humble spirit, to revive the spirit of the humble, and to revive the heart of the contrite ones'" (Isa. 57:15). That's an incredible thought—that God would dwell within a humble person. (See also Colossians 1:27; Galatians 2:20; Philippians 2:13.)

God also promises to hear the "cry" of the humble (Ps. 9:12; 2 Chron. 7:14). Moses "was very humble, more than all men who were on the face of the earth" (Num. 12:3), and he became one of the most renowned men the world has ever known. Godly humility should never be equated with weakness. To be humble is not to become a doormat to the world. True humility is laying down self-will and rebellion and determining to go God's way. It happens in us when we simply say to God, "Jesus, I receive You into my life. Come into my entire being."

I don't like to think of myself as a rebellious person and probably would never have accepted the idea had God not shown it to me. I think of rebellion as an overt act, but it is actually so subtle that most of us fail to see it in our own lives. For many years I failed to see that I very much considered my views to be the only right ones. Looking back, I can see it in the way I spoke to my wife, in the way I thought about church government, in the way I felt about my education, and even in my attitudes toward my giftings. I was definitely a candidate for circumcision and simply could not see it. But God could, and although I felt a strong call to ministry, He disallowed it until He had begun working in me both to will and to do of His good pleasure, which has now become my pleasure too (Phil. 2:13).

This issue of heart circumcision is so vital to our understanding of God's redemption plan that I want to further explore the subject in the next chapter.

CHAPTER 10

Circumcision of the Heart

And the LORD your God will circumcise your hearts and the hearts of your descendants, to love the LORD your God with all your heart and with all your soul, that you may live.

—DEUTERONOMY 30:6

QUESTIONS ABOUT THE necessity of physical circumcision rocked the early years of the New Testament church. There were people saying only those who were circumcised according to the custom of Moses could be saved (Acts 15:1). The apostles quickly countered this legalistic message that had little or nothing to do with true holiness and righteousness. Those teachers had elevated the act of physical circumcision and personal performance above right attitudes and the circumcision of the heart.

While physical circumcision is no longer necessary in covenanting with God, heart circumcision is. In reality circumcision of the heart is equally important on both sides of the cross. Physical circumcision in the Old Testament was intended to be an outward sign of what was happening inwardly. God has always wanted hearts that desired Him. A careful look at the Old Testament reveals that God was always looking for heart circumcision, as Deuteronomy 10:16 proclaims, "Therefore circumcise the foreskin of your heart, and be stiff-necked no longer." (See also Jeremiah 4:4; Romans 2:28–29.)

WHAT CIRCUMCISION MEANS TODAY

In the New Testament era putting away the "works of the flesh" parallels the cutting away of physical flesh in Old Testament times. To avoid confusion about the things that need to be removed, God provides a list: "Now the works of the flesh are evident, which are: adultery, fornication, uncleanness, lewdness, idolatry, sorcery, hatred, contentions, jealousies, outbursts of wrath, selfish ambitions, dissensions, heresies, envy, murders, drunkenness, revelries, and the like" (Gal. 5:19–21). New Testament circumcision of the heart is no less serious than the Old Testament circumcision of the flesh.

A person can do very little to clean up his or her life. Only God can truly clean us up.[1] He knows that human effort alone cannot succeed against the flesh, and He offers His help and strength to face any challenge we encounter in the cleansing process. So then just as a newborn baby cannot circumcise himself, neither can we circumcise our own mind and heart. The Bible tells us, "In Him you were also circumcised with the circumcision made without hands, by putting off the body of the sins of the flesh, by the circumcision of Christ" (Col. 2:11).

The difficulty of putting away sinful things is overcome only by the power of Christ dwelling in us. It is God who works in us "both to will and to do for His good pleasure" (Phil. 2:13). God works through His Spirit inside us for righteousness sake (Gal. 4:6). None of us are capable of putting to death the works of the flesh. None of us find it easy to consistently do what is right. None of us are blameless when it comes to following the Scriptures. God's solution to human weakness is the presence of Jesus within a person's heart. It is literally, "Christ in you, the hope of glory" (Col. 1:27).

God's message in both the Old and New Testaments is that "the LORD your God will circumcise your heart and the heart of your descendants, to love the LORD your God with all your heart and with all your soul, that you may live" (Deut. 30:6). Notice the words "God will circumcise your heart." This means God will complete what we cannot do in our own strength. All that is needed is a willingness to change. He will do nothing without a person's consent. This is the first step in walking in true holiness.

All of this may sound simplistic, and you may wonder, "How do I appropriate God's strength in my life?" Of course, as with many things, there is a learning curve involved, and the change may come gradually. Here is a real-life example. Imagine someone has just cut you off in traffic or offended you in some other way. You are angry, and your emotions start to rise. You would like to get even or at least register some kind of complaint. Then you remember that you've invited Christ to live in you. At first you may feel like praying, "Dear Lord, please turn Your back for just thirty seconds. That's all I ask, just thirty seconds."

Instead, because of the work God's Spirit is doing in your heart, you pray something such as this: "Father, my emotions are ready to explode. I need Your help. I need Your strength. I'm calling on You right now to help settle me down before I make a mistake." You might be surprised at how effective such a prayer can be. Try it! You might also want to recognize that the Scriptures teach that in Christ we are dead to sin. That means that in our anger we don't have to sin. The Scriptures also teach that we can be angry without sinning (Eph. 4:26).

Heart circumcision results in a new creation (Gal 6:15). The man or woman whose heart is circumcised is not only a different person; he or she also becomes "new." According to 2 Corinthians 5:17, "If anyone is in Christ, he is a *new* creation; old things have passed away; behold, all things have become *new*" (emphasis added). The new covenant in Jesus refashions a person back into God's image and likeness. This is not to suggest that a person is cloned into someone he doesn't want to be. On the contrary, *he is changed* into what he was originally intended to be—a person so much better it is inconceivable that anyone would for a moment think of going back to the old person. (We will look at the change that is affected in us through Christ in the last two chapters of this book.)

Before we go on, consider a question. Why was the cutting away of a part of the male sex organ used to illustrate dealing with the flesh? Why not a small slice of the tongue or a part of the hand? Certainly these two parts of the body represent major areas of potential sin. Martin Luther answers this question clearly: "Thus God has betimes taught everyone in circumcision that no one can become pious through works or the Law, and all works and labor to become pious or saved are in vain as long as human nature and the person are not renewed. If, then, He had commanded the hand or the tongue to be circumcised, this would have been an indication that the fault lay in the words and works, that He is favorably disposed toward the nature and the person and hates only the words and the works. But now, since He takes that member which performs no other work than the procreation of human nature and personal being, He makes it clear that the fault lies in the entire essence of human nature, that its birth and entire origin is corrupt and sinful."[2]

CRUCIFYING THE FLESH

A person who has experienced true heart circumcision crucifies the flesh. The Bible says, "For we are the circumcision, who worship God in the Spirit, rejoice in Christ Jesus, and have no confidence in the flesh" (Phil. 3:3). "And those who are Christ's have crucified the flesh with its passions and desires" (Gal. 5:24). Verses like these have a lot to say about having a casual attitude toward righteousness. It is dangerous to presume upon God's grace by allowing it to become a license to sin. Even if His grace covered an indifferent approach toward evil, there would still be problems. First, sin has destructive consequences and in itself destroys lives. Second, sin opens doors to satanic influence.

Confusion develops when we desire to please God in holiness and righteousness but are not always sure of how to accomplish His will. It takes time to mature in the things of the Lord. This initial lack of understanding usually looks to both self-righteousness and works to accomplish salvation. It's as if we say, "We'll prove to God and others that we are truly Christians by the way we live. And we won't compromise like others do."

However, when we observe what some consider a heart-circumcised life (you may want to call it a holy, sanctified, godly, or consecrated life), we often shake our heads. Thirty years ago in some American churches a major emphasis was placed on the length of a woman's skirt, the length of a man's hair, whether women wore makeup and earrings, and numerous other things related to dress codes. Were these things important? Perhaps some were, but eventually most were discarded. Many of those same churches no longer make these things an issue, and they dropped many of them without sacrificing holiness and righteousness.

Today there are still legalistic churches that major in various minors. The real issue is the legislation of their legalism. The demand isn't toward a code of ethics only, which is worthless outside of the indwelling Christ, but a forced demand for allegiance to leadership. Any question or difficulty with authority is met with an accusation that the person with the concern is rebellious. Certainly there are lifestyles that must be dealt with by church leadership. No one in a biblically based body of believers has the right to practice adultery, fornication, homosexuality, or any other scripturally forbidden behavior without expecting to be disciplined. The condemnation of sins the Bible speaks of is not legalism; it is righteousness.

Another real problem with legalism is that it has a tendency to place unrealistic and unscriptural demands on people, which opens the door to a number of other problems. The first is a kind of pride that makes a person feel good about his or her commitment and lifestyle. A telltale sign that pride is at work is a lack of emphasis on Jesus as the source of their ability to maintain a truly righteous life. The second is an attitude of exclusivism. The claim "we are the only true church because of the way we do things" may not be said outright, but it permeates legalistic and self-righteous attitudes. Third, many, especially the youth of legalistic movements, find it increasingly difficult to deal with rebellion. They may hold the line for a while, often wholeheartedly supporting what they are taught, but if and when they do rebel, they often go far beyond typical rebellion. And fourth, legalism creates a phobic kind of fear of God, one far different from the "respect" found in the fear of the Lord.

SEPARATING FROM THE WORLD

God's process of preparing a people for Himself requires the removal of all that is contrary to His nature. Influences generated by both human and satanic rebellion must be cut off by way of separation. Separation allows God's Spirit to influence and regenerate the human spirit. The Bible tells us, "Come out from among them and be separate, says the Lord. Do not touch what is unclean, and I will receive you" (2 Cor. 6:17). But separation, especially from worldly influence, doesn't mean isolation. Jesus said, "I do not pray that You should take them out of the world, but that You should keep them from the evil one. They are not of the world, just as I am not of the world" (John 17:15–16).

Misunderstanding God's intent in this matter drives some to basically reject all contact with those in the world around them. Certainly there is a need to be on guard against worldly influences, but not out of fear or with an attitude of suspicion, arrogance, and pride. This was not the lifestyle Jesus modeled, nor does it line up with what He taught about being in the world but not of the world (John 15:19). Christ's commands about being light and salt in this dark and tasteless world also included a directive to pay taxes ("Render therefore to Caesar the things that are Caesar's, and to God the things that are God's," Matt. 22:21; see also vv. 15–22), and we have been instructed to submit to human government ("Therefore submit yourselves to every ordinance of man for the Lord's sake," 1 Pet. 2:13) and pray for those who rule over us ("Therefore I exhort first of all that supplications, prayers, intercessions, and giving of thanks be made for all men, for kings and all who are in authority, that we may lead a quiet and peaceable life in all godliness and reverence," 1 Tim. 2:1–2).

Jesus Himself hung out with tax collectors and sinners and even helped a Samaritan woman living in sin. The separation God requires is a separation from the sins of the flesh, which in some cases does require limited or restricted contact with some people. The Bible also tells us to separate from believers who are found to be practicing sinful lifestyles.

> I wrote to you in my epistle not to keep company with sexually immoral people. Yet I certainly did not mean with the sexually immoral people of this world, or with the covetous, or extortioners, or idolaters, since then you would need to go out of the world. But now I have written to you not to keep company with anyone named a brother, who is sexually immoral, or covetous, or an idolater, or a reviler, or a drunkard, or an extortioner—not even to eat with such a person. For what have I to do with judging those also who are outside? Do you not judge those who are inside? But those who are outside God judges. Therefore "put away from yourselves the evil person."
>
> —1 Corinthians 5:9–13

I imagine it is safe to say that anyone who has ever desired to model true holiness has at some point wanted to run away from the world. But Paul's admonition in 1 Corinthians 5 was not to run. Rather, he exhorted us to be so filled with the Holy Spirit that we are "insulated" from the world, not "isolated" from it. But again, Paul was adamant against any kind of close fellowship with anyone who called himself a believer but knowingly lived an unscriptural lifestyle.

What then are we to do when a believer is living in sin? First, we must affirm God's grace and His willingness to forgive sin. Yet while God extends His grace to that person, He does so on the basis of confession and repentance, so that person must forsake sin in order to be right with Him. Confession is owning up to the problem, but repentance is walking away from it. God wants us to walk away from sin.

What, you ask, about the person, perhaps a new believer, who is trying to walk away from sin but occasionally falls back into old ways? God recognizes the troubles we have with sin. Therefore, He continues to make His grace available. Again, "If we confess our sins, He is faithful and just to forgive us our sins and to cleanse us from all unrighteousness" (1 John 1:9). Make no mistake; God's grace does not cover "practicing sin." When a person knowingly continues to do what is wrong, especially practicing sin as a lifestyle, he removes himself from God's protection and blessing, as Psalm 66:18 says, "If I regard iniquity in my heart, the Lord will not hear."

Generally it is easy to tell the difference between those who are wrestling with sin and want to do better and those who are in rebellion against God's Word. In most cases attitude defines the difference. The brother or sister who keeps messing up but cries from the heart for help is worlds apart from the person who, with a degree of callousness, always tries to justify his or her sin.

Should we continue to love people who are living in sin? Absolutely! But they need to know that we cannot, according to Scripture, share the close fellowship that belongs to those who walk in the light. They also need to know that we will not listen to the lie that we are to forgive when no real confession and repentance has taken place. Nor will we believe the lie that Christians are loveless, biased, hypocritical people because we condemn sin. That doesn't mean we shun them as some cultures do or that we talk about them among our friends. We pray that they return to right fellowship with God and avail ourselves to minister the truth to them in love when the opportunity arises. For me it is not enough to be "right." No matter how they live, I want everyone to know that I love and care for them.

CHAPTER 11

God's Redemption Plan

*And according to the law almost all things are
purified with blood, and without shedding of
blood there is no remission [forgiveness].*

—Hebrews 9:22

T HE BIBLE IS, for the most part, the story of redemption,
which simply means "to buy back." Mankind chose to
break relationship with God and go his own way, and God in
His love chose to offer reconciliation. The only thing stopping
the reunion was the debt incurred by mankind's sin and the
effect of that sin upon the entire creation.

In Scripture the person paying someone else's debt is called
a "redeemer." The redeemer is, in fact, "buying back" something that had been taken or lost from its rightful place. In
some cases he was redeeming the debtor from an offended
party. The Book of Ruth contains a wonderful account of
redemption. It is the love story of Ruth and Boaz. Boaz was
willing to buy back the property of Ruth's mother-in-law,
Naomi, in order to marry Ruth and have a son to continue
the family line.[1]

The concept of redemption was well understood in the Old
Testament. Job said, "For I know that my Redeemer lives,
and He shall stand at last on the earth" (Job 19:25). David
declared, "Let the words of my mouth and the meditation of
my heart be acceptable in Your sight, O LORD my strength
and my Redeemer" (Ps. 19:14). Isaiah proclaimed, "As for
our Redeemer, the LORD of hosts is His name, the Holy
One of Israel" (Isa. 47:4). These verses and others point to

God Himself as the one willing to personally pay the price to redeem us. This becomes significant when we realize the impossibility of finding a person qualified to pay the debt for human sin.

PAYING THE PRICE

The payment for a debt was called the "ransom."[2] Once the ransom was paid, the offended party was said to be "propitiated,"[3] that is, his anger was now appeased. However, our broken covenant with God would have to be satisfied according to the terms of the original agreement. As we've discussed, the blood covenant requires that the offending party pay for breaking the covenant with his life. This is, for the most part, the nature of all blood covenants, and those who enter into such covenants understand the implication.

Because of this requirement, the ransom would have to be the life of the offending party or the life of someone willing to take his place. That substitute could not owe a debt himself, which was a huge problem since the entire human race had broken covenant with God through sin.[4] Everyone needed a redeemer. In the words of the prophet Isaiah, "But we are all like an unclean thing, and all our righteousnesses are like filthy rags; we all fade as a leaf, and our iniquities, like the wind, have taken us away" (Isa. 64:6).

There was no one to take my place or your place, not a best friend, a parent, or a pastor. Every person alive has done something that violated mankind's covenant relationship with God. That's why God seems distant to many. That's why so many people are unhappy. That's why we go from one thing to another trying to find something to satisfy. That's why our world is a mess.

Finding a worthy substitute would prove to be an impossible task. Even if a candidate could be found, what would compel him to give his life to pay someone else's debt? And even if one substitute could be found, it would still be impossible to find enough substitutes to pay the ransom for all the covenant breakers. Because of the terrible predicament mankind found himself in, God stepped forward and offered to be the Redeemer by way of substitution. Through Jesus the debt could be satisfied once and for all. "Therefore, in all things He had to be made like His brethren, that He might be a merciful and faithful High Priest in things pertaining to God, to make propitiation for the sins of the people" (Heb. 2:17).

Jesus became our substitute. As evangelist D. L. Moody said, "He [Jesus] did not come to buy us from Satan, but from the penalty of our sin."[5] Jesus came to buy out the debt we owed God.

God was willing to pay the price that would appease His own anger. But for reasons known only to Him, He delayed the actual redemption payment until the cross. In the meantime He established the old covenant law to make mankind aware of the seriousness of sin and of the fact that someday the debt resulting from sin would have to be paid in full.

When the time was just right, God sent the promised Messiah to end our indebtedness: "For it pleased the Father that in Him all the fullness should dwell, and by Him to reconcile all things to Himself, by Him, whether things on earth or things in heaven, having made peace through the blood of His cross" (Col. 1:19–20). As New Testament Greek scholar Kenneth Wuest explains, "The Messiah found and procured salvation by means of His outpoured blood. This is also told us in the Greek word translated 'redemption,' *lutrosis*. The verb form of this word means 'to release on receipt of ransom, to redeem or liberate by payment of a ransom.'"[6]

A TEMPORARY SOLUTION

While waiting for full redemption through Jesus, God allowed sin to be "covered" or "hidden" from His sight by the shedding of innocent animal blood. God's universal principle is that only blood can atone for sin. A person had to face the sobering consequences of his sin as he watched an innocent animal die in his place.

As strange as it may sound, God initiated a system that He Himself did not like. David expressed the matter as God revealed it to him: "For You do not desire sacrifice, or else I would give it; You do not delight in burnt offering. The sacrifices of God are a broken spirit, a broken and a contrite heart—these, O God, You will not despise" (Ps. 51:16–17). The sacrificial system was temporary and pointed to the final substitute who was yet to come.

While animal blood only "covered" or "shielded" a person's sin from God's anger, there needed to be something more permanent to dispel the constant reminder of sin. "But in those sacrifices [the blood that covered the sin] there is a reminder of sins every year" (Heb. 10:3). To enjoy any lasting peace of mind, sin would have to be dealt with once and for all. When sin is dealt with completely, the penalty is canceled along with the guilt and shame.[7]

Many Christians live much of their lives in dread of losing their salvation. It is more difficult to fall out of favor with God than some are led to believe. The blood covenant bond is strong and breaking covenant with God has more to do with the motives of the heart than with actions. Certainly actions are important—very important—but notice what God says about the heart: "For out of the heart proceed evil thoughts, murders, adulteries, fornications, thefts, false witness, blasphemies" (Matt. 15:19). And, "Therefore I was angry with that generation, and said, 'They always go astray in their heart, and they have not known My ways'" (Heb. 3:10).

Sin begins in our hearts. Judas probably struggled before he decided to betray Christ. While it was still a thought—a temptation he had not yielded to—there was no sin. The moment he said yes to his dark thoughts, embracing them in his heart, he broke covenant with God and exiled himself from God's blessings and protection. (See Luke 22:3–4.)

The heart is where sin occurs, and only God truly knows the heart. This is one reason it is often difficult to truly know where another person stands spiritually, "for man looks at the outward appearance, but the LORD looks at the heart" (1 Sam. 16:7).

CHAPTER 12

The Power of Substitution

*But into the second part the high priest went alone once
a year, not without blood, which he offered for himself
and for the people's sins committed in ignorance.*

—HEBREWS 9:7

A s DISCUSSED IN the previous chapter, Jesus would become
our substitute and end our indebtedness once and for all.
Briefly we need to expound on the concept of substitution.
Knowing that He would use a divine substitute to redeem
mankind from sin, God gave many illustrations of substitution
at work through the Scriptures.

In the Book of Genesis God taught Abraham the principle of substitution in two ways. First, God used the substitutionary blood of animals when establishing His covenant with
him, as we discussed in chapter 4. (See Genesis 15:17–18.) The
second lesson came many years later when Abraham's promised
child, Isaac, was a boy. God told Abraham to go to a distant
mountain and sacrifice Isaac. Abraham obediently left the next
morning with the young man, climbed the mountain, prepared
the altar, bound Isaac, and placed him on the altar. But as he
raised his knife to slay his son, God called out and stopped
Abraham. Then He provided a ram to take Isaac's place as the
sacrifice. (See Genesis 22:1–14.)

We also see the principle of substitution during Moses's day.
God commanded Moses to bring Him two goats. Aaron was
then instructed to "cast lots for the goats: one lot for the LORD
and the other lot for the scapegoat. And Aaron shall bring the
goat on which the LORD's lot fell, and offer it as a sin offering.

But the goat on which the lot fell to be the scapegoat shall be presented alive before the LORD, to make atonement upon it, and to let it go as the scapegoat into the wilderness" (Lev. 16:8–10).

Both goats present a picture of substitution. The first goat, which was killed, dramatically demonstrated that the people's sin had to be paid for in blood. Through the second goat, the scapegoat, the sins of the people were symbolically removed and driven out into the wilderness never to be seen again. Again God's message was clear: someone or something had to pay for sin. The only way for His people to escape the penalty of sin was for that penalty (death) to be laid upon another— a substitute. "So Christ was offered once to bear the sins of many" (Heb. 9:28).

Job also was a man who well understood the necessity of atonement (compensation, making amends) by way of a substitute. Fearing his children had sinned grievously against God, Job would "rise early in the morning and offer burnt offerings according to the number of them all. For Job said, 'It may be that my sons have sinned and cursed God in their hearts.' Thus Job did regularly" (Job 1:5).

Last, I want to share a slightly more recent example of substitution. In his book *The Blood Covenant* H. Clay Trumbull recounts a story about nineteenth-century explorer and journalist Henry Morton Stanley that paints a vivid picture of this principle at work. In a covenant-making ceremony in Africa Stanley joined himself to Itsi, king of Ntamo, by way of a blood covenant.

> "The treaty with Itsi," says Stanley, "was exceedingly ceremonious, and involved the exchange of charms. Itsi transferred to me for my protection through life, a small gourdful of a curious powder, which had rather a saline taste; and I delivered over to him, as the white man's charm against all evil, a half-ounce vial of magnesia; further, a small scratch in Frank's arm, and another in Itsi's

arm, supplied blood sufficient to unite us in one, and [by an] indivisible bond of fraternity."[1]

In Stanley's own words we find that one of his men, Frank Pocock, substituted his blood for Stanley's. According to Trumbull, this was not unusual, especially among individuals of a high rank. Trumbull goes on to describe what happened years later after Frank Pocock had died.

Four years later Stanley found himself back at Ntamo. However, by this time Frank Pocock had died, and Itsi was barbaric enough to cause Stanley much concern. Would the covenant hold? Or would Itsi consider it invalid because Frank's blood had been substituted for his and Frank was now dead? Stanley knew this African chieftain was no one to fool with.

> "My brother being the supreme lord of Ntamo, as well as the deepest-voiced and most arrogant rogue among the whole tribe," says Stanley, "first demanded the two asses [which Stanley had with him], then a large mirror, which was succeeded by a splendid gold-embroidered coat, jewelry, glass clasps, long brass chains, a figure table-cloth, fifteen other pieces of fine cloth, and a japanned tin box with a 'Chubb' lock. Finally, gratified by such liberality, Ngalyema surrendered to me his scepter, which consisted of a long staff, banded profusely with brass, and decorated with coils of brass wire, which was to be carried by me and shown to all men that I was the brother of Ngalyema [or, Itsi] of Ntamo!" Some time after this, when trouble arose between Stanley and Ngalyema, the former suggested that perhaps it would be better to cancel their brotherhood. "'No, no, no,'" cried Ngalyema, anxiously; 'our brotherhood cannot be broken; our blood is now one.'" Yet at this time Stanley's brotherhood with Ngalyema was only by the blood of his deceased retainer, Frank Pocock.[2]

Thus the covenant held even though Stanley used someone else's blood in making it. This is the same picture painted earlier when God used animal blood for His part of making blood covenant with Abraham. Animal blood was a substitute in making a full blood covenant with Abraham. And Jesus's blood would become the substitute for ours in making atonement for our sins.

CHAPTER 13

Passover: Commemorating the Old Covenant

By faith he kept the Passover and the sprinkling of blood,
lest he who destroyed the firstborn should touch them.

—HEBREWS 11:28

WHEN THE CHILDREN of Israel prepared to leave Egypt to return to the land of Canaan, Pharaoh prevented them from doing so. Numerous times they tried to leave and each time were met with resistance from the Egyptians. In response God finally determined to severely discipline Egypt with a plague that would kill the firstborn of every household. Through Moses God instructed the people of Israel to protect themselves from the approaching death plague by renewing their covenant with Him. When the death angel passed over the land, only those in blood covenant with God would be spared.

Moses instructed each household to take a male lamb without blemish and kill it at twilight. Then they were to "take some of the blood and put it on the two doorposts and on the lintel of the houses where they eat it" (Exod. 12:7). And God said, "Now the blood shall be a sign for you on the houses where you are. And when I see the blood, I will pass over you; and the plague shall not be on you to destroy you when I strike the land of Egypt" (v. 13).

Notice that God said, "Now the blood shall be a sign for you." We see again here that blood served as the signature on an agreement with God.

In the very next verse God commanded the Israelites to

remember that day: "So this day shall be to you a memorial; and you shall keep it as a feast to the Lord throughout your generations. You shall keep it as a feast by an everlasting ordinance" (v. 14). This would be called Passover. It was to be a day of remembering, a permanent memorial to remind the people that they were in blood covenant with God.[1]

It is worth noting that God required a specific sacrifice for Passover: a lamb (vv. 21–27). The Passover sacrifice was not like the sin offerings that addressed disobedience. The blood of the Passover lamb was used in "making" agreements, not for making payments for broken agreements. Thus the Passover offering was designed to reinstate and remember blood covenant with God, as the blood of the Passover lamb represented both blessing and protection for Israel.

On that first Passover the application of the blood to the lintel (support) and doorposts of the house was symbolic of the application of blood in the forming of a covenant. Thus the Israelite was saying with each stroke of the hyssop branch, "I am in covenant with You, God." If, however, Israel failed to fulfill their covenant with God, their fate would have been the same as the Egyptians'.

While Israel's physical obedience brought them deliverance on that occasion, the real issue was, and still is, heart obedience. Remember again that circumcision of the heart involves laying down rebellion against God through a broken and contrite heart: "Circumcise yourselves to the Lord, and take away the foreskins of your hearts, you men of Judah and inhabitants of Jerusalem, lest My fury come forth like fire, and burn so that no one can quench it, because of the evil of your doings" (Jer. 4:4).

Modern Jews continue to observe Passover to commemorate their deliverance from Egyptian bondage. But none, Jew or Gentile, should forget that this ordinance commemorates not only deliverance but also covenant. Passover is a reminder not only of our relationship with God but also of what He has done for us in paying for broken covenants. It should also serve as a powerful reminder that obedience through Jesus is necessary in order for His blood to protect us.

As the Israelites found protection only as they remained in their homes where the blood had been applied to the doorway, so believers find that Christ's blood shelters those who abide in a living relationship with Him. Sloppy living and ignorance of the importance of blood in a covenant relationship give the enemy of our souls access to our lives. This thief comes for nothing "except to steal, and to kill, and to destroy." Jesus, on the other hand, came "that they may have life, and that they may have it more abundantly" (John 10:10).

CHAPTER 14

The Signature of the New Covenant

In the same manner He also took the cup after supper, saying, "This cup is the new covenant in My blood. This do, as often as you drink it, in remembrance of Me."

—1 Corinthians 11:25

THE STIPULATIONS OF the Mosaic agreement, specifically the Law, remained intact for hundreds of years. God did not start over again with each succeeding generation, giving new and different conditions every time a covenant was made. The Ten Commandments became emblazoned upon the Jewish mind as the commandments of God, good for every age. This is consistent with a God who does not change.

Little did those under the Law realize but that laws concerning righteousness, then carved on tablets of stone, would eventually be written on the fleshly tablets of the human heart. (See Hebrews 8:10; Jeremiah 31:33–34.)

There is nothing so difficult to deal with than to be given a free will and ultimately find a host of things that hinder it, especially rules and laws. While the principles of righteousness remained external in the embodiment of the Law, in a manner of speaking those principles got in the way of free will. This, of course, would not have been a problem if Adam's "original" free will had not come under the influence of sin. If Adam had chosen correctly in the first place, he would never have had a later problem with his ability to choose.

The Law then was good in that it alerted humanity to potential problems with choices. But it could not, in itself, make people righteous. After Adam sinned, he had no fountain of life from within, no internal resource of power, no real motivation for righteousness, and no personal relationship with God. God's solution for Adam's problem was to change the manner in which righteousness was to be administered.

This new administration had to come through a renewed personal relationship with God. No one was capable of keeping the Law. Thus the covenant was always in jeopardy. If God and mankind could unite on some basis other than the Law, the future wouldn't be dictated by the demands of the Law; it would now be upheld through the indwelling Christ. At the same time righteousness and holiness would have to be upheld. God would not form an association with anyone living contrary to His character and personality, which is manifest through the Law.

The plan was ingenious and would involve the commingling of God's Spirit with the human spirit. Christ's Spirit would literally come to abide in any person who would allow Him to do so. The result would be Christ working from within "both to will and to do of His good pleasure" (Phil. 2:13). Only through Christ could the fulfillment of righteousness be inscribed upon the human heart so that it would manifest itself in sincere and genuine spontaneous actions. Only the indwelling Christ could give the strength to live a righteous life.

God designed the old covenant to eventually end in order for a new covenant to begin. The Bible says, "For on the one hand there is an annulling of the former commandment because of its weakness and unprofitableness" (Heb. 7:18). And, "In that He says, 'A new covenant,' He has made the first obsolete. Now what is becoming obsolete and growing old is ready to vanish away" (Heb. 8:13).

When the old covenant was replaced with the new, there were no more sacrifices or sin offerings, no more earthly high priests and temples of stone. Now the gospel was preached and holiness was created from within through God's Spirit, who is our helper, comforter, and healer.

The old agreement was a "schoolmaster" to lead to the new agreement, literally to Christ Himself, as the apostle Paul wrote: "Therefore the law was our tutor to bring us to Christ, that we might be justified by faith" (Gal. 3:24). Only Christ's presence in a person's life could empower him or her to live in a manner consistent with God's design. The entire point of restoration is to bring us back to our original relationship with God, and that relationship involved the uniting of God's Spirit with the human spirit. And Jesus is the only person who could make this happen.

Unlike the old covenant, this new agreement would allow God to work deep within the human spirit to make us righteous. The stress of knowing we could never live up to the demands of the Law could now be turned over to the indwelling Christ. Once the new covenant was in place, God chose men to immediately make known the riches of this new administration, which was the message of the gospel. Paul noted that God had made him a minister "of the new covenant, not of the letter but of the Spirit; for the letter kills, but the Spirit gives life" (2 Cor. 3:6).

Christianity loses its effectiveness when it is seen solely through the eyes of the Law. As long as it remains a list of things to do, it does not have the power for righteous living. Until we learn that living in Christ is the only way to fulfill the righteous demands of the Law, we will constantly be driven by a need to perform, and as a result will have to deal regularly with self-righteousness and pride. As long as a person tries to live the Christian life under the demands of the Law, Christ will be little more than a historical figure who is given mental assent and not heartfelt devotion.

Under the new covenant commandments would no longer stare people in the face "demanding" righteousness. The new order would allow the principles of righteousness engraved in stone to now be personally obeyed through Christ or, again, to be written on the human heart. That's why Paul wrote, "Clearly you are an epistle of Christ, ministered by us, written not with ink but by the Spirit of the living God, not on tablets of stone but on tablets of flesh, that is, of the heart" (2 Cor. 3:3). A person under the new agreement would literally find himself desiring to do good as God worked within him.

THE SIGNING OF THE NEW COVENANT

This transfer to the administration of righteousness did not take place where most people tend to believe it did. Ask anyone where the new covenant began, and most will say it was on the cross. Yet as important as the cross of Christ is to salvation, it is not the place where the new covenant was "signed," or put into effect. How could the cross be the initiation of the agreement when, in fact, it represents the payment for broken agreements? Remember, blood covenants are first "made" (signed) in blood and then, if failed, are to be "paid" for in blood. The cross was where payment for our sins was made.

The new covenant was actually signed when the disciples celebrated the Passover with Jesus just prior to His death. While the men were gathered with Him in the Upper Room for the annual celebration, Jesus initiated the new agreement.

> And as they were eating, Jesus took bread, blessed it and broke it, and gave it to the disciples and said, "Take, eat; this is my body." Then He took the cup, and gave thanks, and gave it to them, saying, "Drink from it, all of you. For this is My blood of the new covenant, which is shed for many for the remission of sins."
>
> —MATTHEW 26:26–28

Two tremendous things happen in these few sentences. First, God shows that He is about to prove, beyond question, His incredible love for humanity at Calvary. The breaking of the body of Jesus, who is literally God, would forever settle any potential controversy over God's love. God descending from heaven to suffer the pain that touches all of humanity would prove that He not only understood what we face but also cared about our suffering.

Second, by way of substitution God used the blood of the grape to symbolize His own blood in making the agreement. In a previous chapter we saw that substitutionary blood was acceptable in making agreements. God ordained this unique meeting in the Upper Room for the purpose of making a blood covenant with anyone willing to covenant with Him. It wasn't just the disciples Jesus was appealing to. It was all of humanity.

However, in contrast to the way things were done in the Old Testament, God manifested Himself in the person of Jesus Christ in making the new covenant. This time He would not pass as a torch through the bloody parts of an animal as He did when He entered into covenant with Abraham. This time He would appear in person. As Bible teacher Ray Stedman observed:

> "On the night in which he was betrayed, Jesus took a cup of wine, passed it to his disciples and said: 'Drink from it, all of you. This is my blood of the covenant, which is poured out for many for the forgiveness of sins'" (Mt 26:27–28). With those words and that symbolic action, he borrowed the phrase used by Moses when he took the blood of an animal, sprinkled it on the people and said, "This is the blood of the covenant that the LORD has made with you in accordance with all these words" (Ex 24:8). The contrast was deliberate. Moses used the blood of an animal; Jesus used wine as a symbol of his own blood.[1]

In the Book of Genesis there is a prophetic reference to this Upper Room event and to the cross. Near the end of Jacob's life he called his twelve sons together to tell them what would befall them in the last days (Gen. 49:1). He told Judah, "The scepter shall not depart from Judah, nor a lawgiver from between his feet, until Shiloh comes; and to him shall be the obedience of the people. *Binding his donkey to the vine, and his donkey's colt to the choice vine, he washed his garments in wine, and his clothes in the blood of grapes"* (vv. 10–11, emphasis added).

The terminology in this verse is not accidental; it is a direct reference to the events leading up to and including the cross. The donkey Jesus rode into Jerusalem was on God's mind hundreds of years before the event took place. And the reference to the "blood of grapes" was God's way of telling us that this event was planned well in advance to initiate a powerful relationship with mankind.

Follow carefully the words of Jesus to fully understand what happened in the Upper Room. Referring to the cup, Jesus says, "Drink from it, all of you. For this [the cup of the grape] is [represents] My blood of the new covenant" (Matt. 26:27–28). We are not privileged to know why Jesus did not follow customary Jewish procedures for making the agreement by using actual blood. It appears, however, that the disciples were familiar with covenant making and recognized immediately what Jesus was doing, and in this way they knowingly entered into the agreement.

Later the apostle Paul, pointing to the cup used in the Upper Room, reminded us of Jesus's words: "This cup is the new covenant in My blood" (1 Cor. 11:25). Here the blood of grapes is understood to be a substitute for real blood in making the agreement. Although the symbol, which is usually actual blood, is important, the primary issue was that regardless of whether the blood was real or substitutionary, the results were the same.

This was a blood covenant just as powerful as any blood covenant ever made, and it embodied all the rights, privileges, and responsibilities of such an agreement. In the Upper Room the agreement was made with substitutionary blood with the understanding that if it was broken, the debt was to be paid in blood.

The seriousness of the covenant seems to be on Peter's mind when Jesus predicts that the disciples will ultimately fail to honor Him. Peter is quick to tell Jesus, "Even if all are made to stumble because of You, I will never be made to stumble" (Matt. 26:33). He quickly reaffirms his commitment by saying, "Even if I have to die with You, I will not deny you" (v. 35), and it seems at this point the rest of the disciples commit to do the same. They knew they had entered into a binding agreement and had every intention of living up to their end of the bargain, because as we saw previously, all covenants have stipulations.

CHAPTER 15

The Stipulations of the New Covenant

But if we walk in the light as He is in the light, we have fellowship with one another, and the blood of Jesus Christ His Son cleanses us from all sin.

—1 JOHN 1:7

THE SCRIBES AND Pharisees, who were Jewish religious leaders, were concerned about what Jesus believed and taught concerning the Law. Had He come to destroy it, or did He just want to bend it a little to fit His own agenda? Most of their concern may have involved the fear of losing their influence as guardians of the Law. Jesus responded to their questions authoritatively. "Do not think that I came to destroy the Law or the Prophets. I did not come to destroy but to fulfill. For assuredly, I say to you, till heaven and earth pass away, one jot or one tittle will by no means pass from the law till all is fulfilled" (Matt. 5:17–18).

According to the Book of Hebrews, when the Law was "fulfilled," or when it had completed its purpose, it became obsolete. That means it was no longer of any use. "In that He says, 'A new covenant,' He has made the first obsolete. Now what is becoming obsolete and growing old is ready to vanish away" (Heb. 8:13). The new law in Christ, with its "heart" for righteousness, was literally a "replacement," one that God had in mind from the very beginning and one that would better the first.

There are basically two problems associated with our understanding of this change in covenants. There are some who think that by saying the Law is obsolete, Scripture is saying its stipulations are no longer in effect. And then there are those who do not understand how the new covenant fulfilled the Law and therefore think it is in effect today just as it was before Christ. Both positions miss the reason the Law was given in the first place and the Christ who came to fulfill it.

THE SIMPLICITY OF COVENANTING WITH GOD

The Law outlined the conditions for entering into a blood covenant with God. Those stipulations remained in effect from the time of Moses, when the Law was put in place, until the formation of the new covenant.[1] If a person wanted to be in union with God, he had to keep the Ten Commandments along with all the other ordinances that made up the Law. While the old covenant stipulations may seem extensive and demanding, Jesus revealed that they were really quite simple. Though there seemed to be dozens of commandments, there were really only two. To be in agreement with God one must abide by only two basic stipulations: he must love God, and he must love others. Jesus said, "On these two commandments hang all the Law and the Prophets" (Matt. 22:40).

However, because of the rebellion in mankind's heart, God had to spell things out in detail, hence the multitude of ordinances. But this is not the entire reason the Law came into existence. The Law was also intended to lead us to Christ, to the perfect man, and to the perfecting of all who would agree to the new covenant. The Law did the leading by showing the unreliability of works as a viable way of establishing true righteousness. Pride boasts, "I can do anything, just watch me," or "I'm as good as anybody else," or "Just tell me what to do, and I'll do it." It doesn't acknowledge a need for God.

God gave the Law, and almost immediately the struggle to fulfill it and other righteous demands became so intense that it actually made people want to give up on right living. Granted, another reason also exists—that of rebellion. But is the Law itself a bad thing? Romans 7:7 begins with the same basic question: "What shall we say then? Is the law sin?" Paul answers, "Certainly not! On the contrary, I would not have known sin except through the law. For I would not have known covetousness unless the law had said, 'You shall not covet.'"

Initially the flesh made alive by the Law tied Paul in knots as he tried to keep the Law. Eventually he cried, "O wretched man that I am! Who will deliver me from this body of death?" (v. 24). He answers his own question in the next verse: "Jesus Christ our Lord" (v. 25).

It sounds too simple—"Jesus is the answer." But that is the truth that so many miss when confronted with the righteous demands of the Law. They struggle trying desperately to perform adequately so God will not be angry with them or so they can believe their salvation is intact. Works (working), though important, never produced an ounce of true righteousness, yet the command is that we be righteous people. How? We are righteous in Christ. Jesus Himself is our entire righteousness. Through faith in Him we have fulfilled the Law. At the same time He is working in us by His Holy Spirit. "Christ in us" is our only hope. It is the only solution for true righteousness. Or in the words of Scripture:

> There is therefore now no condemnation to those who are in Christ Jesus, who do not walk according to the flesh, but according to the Spirit. For the law of the Spirit of life in Christ Jesus has made me free from the law of sin and death. For what the law could not do in that it was weak through the flesh, God did by sending His own Son in the likeness of sinful flesh, on account of sin: He condemned sin in the flesh, that the righteous requirement of the law might be fulfilled in us who do not walk according to the flesh but according to the Spirit.
>
> —ROMANS 8:1–4

That means that no amount of righteousness, which we still need, can be accomplished through personal performance. It is

Jesus who gives "life to the dead" (Rom. 4:17). Keep in mind His words "for without Me you can do nothing" (John 15:5). The concept of developing a godly life through the power of the indwelling Christ runs cross grain to the idea that God has left us on this planet with a set of rules that He will judge us by when He returns. The perception that God sits in heaven with a divine scorecard tallying up good and bad deeds does not take into account the power of the indwelling Christ.

Certainly there is going to be an accounting of the deeds done in the body. But those who discover the impossibility of maintaining a righteous life on their own and then turn to Jesus for the strength only He can provide will experience the beauty of the Christian life. (See 1 Corinthians 1:30.) Their righteousness will be the righteousness of Christ. As they trust in His righteousness, they find that He "is able to do exceedingly abundantly above all that we ask or think, according to the power that works in us" (Eph. 3:20).

Horatius Bonar, a nineteenth-century Scottish minister and poet, wrote, "Faith is the acknowledgment of the entire absence of all goodness in us, and the recognition of the cross as the substitute for all the want on our part. The whole work is His, not ours, from first to last."[2]

Here is where the truth comes alive. On life's freeway people have a tendency to get in one another's way, raising the potential for inappropriate and loveless responses. Anger, resentment, and impatience make people want to force others off the road. Because of the Law they know they shouldn't do this, but they feel powerless to resist the temptation. Again, the Law only promises to reward failure with guilt and shame. It does nothing to equip them to resist the desire to retaliate. This is why not a few have sunk to the depths of hopelessness when their attempts at righteousness were unsuccessful. When, however, they invite Christ to be their strength, they find victory over sin and temptation.

I know many Christians who testify that they could not

control themselves in difficult situations until they literally invited Christ to be their strength. With Christ's help the desire to do wrong was defused, and they were able to find an appropriate response where formerly they would have acted improperly.

ONLY THROUGH CHRIST

The Law showed us what was necessary to please God. It established the measure of true righteousness. But it also exposed our absolute inability to live out its precepts. Paul understood that well when he declared, "For I know that in me (that is, in my flesh) nothing good dwells; for to will is present with me, but how to perform what is good I do not find" (Rom. 7:18).

Look for a moment at righteousness through the eyes of Nehemiah. Notice how he saw personal performance as a means of pleasing God. "Remember me, O my God, concerning this, and do not wipe out my good deeds that I have done for the house of my God, and for its services!" (Neh. 13:14). How wonderful it would have been if he could have looked ahead to see Jesus's sacrifice to make him righteous before God once and for all, but he continued to plead for God to remember his good works. "And I commanded the Levites that they should cleanse themselves, and that they should go and guard the gates, to sanctify the Sabbath day. Remember me, O my God, concerning this also, and spare me according to the greatness of Your mercy!" (v. 22).

Nehemiah knew only the Law and worked hard to live up to its standards. Although he lived by faith, he knew little other than works as a way of pleasing God, and he was somewhat proud of his accomplishments. But no doubt Nehemiah, a man of God, would have confessed his shortcomings like all others who understand that good works fall far short of real goodness.

My intent is not to minimize the need for righteousness and holiness. Just the opposite. My intent is to show that we need God's help through Jesus to accomplish anything that is good.

God used the Law to lead us to Christ. "For what the law could not do in that it was weak through the flesh, God did by sending His own Son in the likeness of sinful flesh, on account of sin: He condemned sin in the flesh" (Rom. 8:3). Let me emphasize this again: God desires to work within a person in order to both give life and to deal with sin. Don't miss this. Yes, for the Christian the dictatorial demands of the Law are gone, but right living is still necessary because sin destroys. Only today, now that the new covenant has been established, Christ's working "in us" brings about that right living. As Christ lives within, a cooperative work allows His righteousness to be manifested. Again, "For it is God who works in you both to will and to do of His good pleasure" (Phil. 2:13). This becomes most evident when a person passes from darkness to light and finds so many things changed inside. One of the predominant features of the Christlike life (or the Christ "in us" life) is the new desire to live a life that is pleasing to God. It isn't the Law demanding this new lifestyle; it is the imprint of Jesus living inside by His Spirit.

KEEPING THE COVENANT

If people would agree to the two stipulations for fulfilling the Law—to love God and to love others—God would agree to two conditions Himself. The Book of Genesis makes it clear that even after the fall God was willing, through covenant, to once again fellowship with mankind. As part of His side of the agreement He first promised to protect mankind from evil and from the enemy of his soul. There are a number of verses in Scripture in which He promises this protection: "Do not be afraid, Abram. I am your shield, your exceedingly great reward" (Gen. 15:1); "As for God, His way is perfect; the word of the LORD is proven; He is a shield to all who trust in Him" (2 Sam. 22:31); "But You, O LORD, are a shield for me, my glory and the One who lifts up my head" (Ps. 3:3).

Second, God guaranteed His blessings: "And I will make

My covenant between Me and you, and will multiply you exceedingly" (Gen. 17:2). Those in covenant with God knew of the blessings He promised. Moses spoke of them: "And all these blessings shall come upon you and overtake you, because you obey the voice of the LORD your God: 'Blessed shall you be in the city, and blessed shall you be in the country. Blessed shall be the fruit of your body, the produce of your ground and the increase of your herds, the increase of your cattle and the offspring of your flocks. Blessed shall be your basket and your kneading bowl. Blessed shall you be when you come in, and blessed shall you be when you go out'" (Deut. 28:2–6). David, Solomon, and Isaiah also spoke of God's blessings: "For You meet him with the blessings of goodness; You set a crown of pure gold upon his head" (Ps. 21:3); "A faithful man will abound with blessings, but he who hastens to be rich will not go unpunished" (Prov. 28:20); "For I will pour water on him who is thirsty, and floods on the dry ground; I will pour My Spirit on your descendants, and My blessing on your offspring" (Isa. 44:3).

God's words to Adam form the basis for our need for His blessing. "Cursed is the ground for your sake; in toil you shall eat of it all the days of your life" (Gen. 3:17). The earth in its present condition is not capable of bringing forth enough to sustain mankind. Only as God blesses the land does it provide for our needs. Compare nations that have acknowledged and served God to those that have not, and the effects on the ground's ability to yield food is evident. It is highly possible that the only reason the ground brings forth anything good is because of God's blessing toward His covenant people.

The second set of stipulations—our part—can, again, be summed up in two commandments: love God and love others. This isn't romantic love; I see it as more a matter of showing honor or respect. So we are to honor and respect God, and we are to honor and respect others. Fortunately we don't even have to love God in our own strength. First John 4:19 tells us, "We love Him because He first loved us."

John also makes the need for obeying the second stipulation (loving others) quite clear: "For this is the message that you heard from the beginning, that you should love one another.... We know that we have passed from death to life, because we love the brethren. He who does not love his brother abides in death. Whoever hates his brother is a murderer, and you know that no murderer has eternal life abiding in him" (1 John 3:11–15). John goes on to say, "And whatever we ask we receive from Him, because we keep His commandments and do those things that are pleasing in His sight. And this is His commandment: that we should believe on the name of His Son Jesus Christ and love one another, as He gave us commandment" (vv. 22–23).

It is just as the apostle Paul declared: "The purpose of the commandment is love from a pure heart, from a good conscience, and from sincere faith" (1 Tim. 1:5).

CHAPTER 16

Washed in Blood

And by Him to reconcile all things to Himself, by Him, whether things on earth or things in heaven, having made peace through the blood of His cross.

—COLOSSIANS 1:20

IN HEAVEN ONE of the elders asked, "Who are these arrayed in white robes, and where did they come from?" John responded, "Sir, you know." The elder continued, "These are the ones who come out of the great tribulation, and *washed their robes and made them white in the blood of the Lamb*" (Rev. 7:13–14, emphasis added).

The Scriptures make it clear that the fabric of human existence is stained by sin and must be cleansed. The Scriptures also make it clear that only Jesus's blood can remove sin: "For he who lacks these things is shortsighted, even to blindness, and has forgotten that he was *cleansed from his old sins*" (2 Pet. 1:9, emphasis added). As noted Bible scholar G. Campbell Morgan declared, the stain of sin "cannot be removed without blood, and that which is infinitely more, and deeper, and profounder, and more terrible than blood, of which blood is but the symbol—the suffering of Deity."[1]

Some people serve God out of fear. They are not as concerned with going to heaven as they are with staying out of hell. Yet to them the responsibilities involved in a covenant relationship with God seem staggering, and they think it impossible to live a righteous life before God. What they don't realize is that goodness requires a relationship with God. Christians are "supposed"[2] to be good people to be a part of God's kingdom.

But those who discover just how hard it is to be good should not cancel themselves out of any hope of truly pleasing God.

As we discussed in the last chapter, only God can empower us to live right before Him. Even salvation comes only by God's grace. It can't be earned, bought, or inherited from our parents, as the Bible proclaims: "Now all things are of God, who has reconciled us to Himself through Jesus Christ, and has given us the ministry of reconciliation, that is, that God was in Christ reconciling the world to Himself" (2 Cor. 5:18–19).

The issue of our goodness coming from God is further clarified in that God extends salvation only on the basis of Jesus's blood. Forgiveness of sin is not arbitrary. It's not God saying, "OK, since I'm God I'll just forget what you've done because I know that you are sorry." God's forgiveness is always based on Jesus's paying the price for our sin with His blood as Ephesians 2:13 says: "But now in Christ Jesus you who once were far off have been made near by the blood of Christ."

Once again this atonement is made possible through the substitutionary blood of Christ shed in His substitutionary death on the cross. So then we have access to God through Jesus, but that access is granted only on the basis of Christ's blood. If Christ had died in another manner, such as by hanging or drowning, salvation would have been incomplete because His death did not save us; His blood did! Numerous verses in Scripture make it clear that only blood can atone for sin. Only by the blood of Jesus can we come to God. Paul wrote, "For it pleased the Father that in Him all the fullness should dwell, and by Him to reconcile all things to Himself, by Him, whether things on earth or things in heaven, having made peace through the blood of His cross" (Col. 1:19–20).

It is easy to think that works and good deeds will get us into God's good graces. But again the Scriptures are straightforward about this: "Not by works of righteousness which we have done, but according to His mercy He saved us, through the washing of regeneration and renewing of the Holy Spirit"

(Titus 3:5). This, of course, doesn't mean there is nothing to do but sit back and wait for Jesus to come. On the contrary, there is much work to be done in this present world—work to do for God's kingdom, but not work to do in order to be saved.

Am I saying we can live any way we please because salvation is granted apart from personal righteousness? Not at all. Paul addresses this question quite plainly in his letter to Titus. After affirming that salvation is apart from works in chapter 3, verse 5, and further affirming that we are justified by nothing other than grace, Paul states in Titus 3:8 that "those who have believed in God should be careful to maintain good works. These things are good and profitable to men." The free gift of salvation and God's incredible grace must never be seen as an open door to sin. Should anyone ask why, the answer is simple: sin diminishes joy, peace, happiness, security, authority, and boldness before God's throne. It further opens doors to the influence of demons and ruins a person's testimony.

ALL HAVE SINNED

Should we be tempted to believe that we have done nothing worthy of death and therefore have no need of a Savior, we should look again at what God expects of us. Once again He asks but two things: to love (which, biblically speaking, means to honor and respect) Him and others. Follow this carefully. The moment we offend or hurt someone, we have violated God's laws and become worthy of death. James confirms this when he says, "If you really fulfill the royal law according to the Scripture, 'You shall love your neighbor as yourself,' you do well; but if you show partiality, you commit sin, and are convicted by the law as transgressors. For whoever shall keep the whole law, and yet stumble in one point, he is guilty of all" (James 2:8–10). Even those who willingly choose to avoid people are breaking the commandment to love others.

Our world is messed up, not because God wants it that way and has willed it to be so, but because of the breaking of these two commandments. Think for a moment about how people treat one another. Better yet, think about how you relate to those around you. How many people have had a bad day because you were having a bad day? How many times have you said or done something you knew would hurt another person? This is what creates the havoc in our world.

You may think, "Sure, I could have been nicer and kinder here or there, but it really wasn't that big of a deal. I didn't kill anybody." The degree of our sin makes no difference. We are still not excused. It's the trillions of "not so bad" acts that have led to more offensive behavior and a world that's in terrible shape. Sadly we blame God instead of ourselves. Why, we ask, does He allow bad things to happen? But God is not the one who has broken covenant; we are. As Proverbs 19:3 says, "The foolishness of a man twists his way, and his heart frets against the LORD."

OUR SINS HAVE BEEN CARRIED AWAY

Our sin sickness would be fatal if not for Jesus. Jesus's blood did more than just cover our sins so that we might be in good standing with God. It completely carried them away. Quite far according to the psalmist—"As far as the east is from the west, so far has He removed our transgressions from us" (Ps. 103:12).

Remember that we discussed in chapter 11 that sin was removed from God's sight at Calvary. Jesus was different from the Old Testament sacrifices, whose blood shielded mankind's sin from God's sight. As the the writer to the Hebrews said, "It is not possible that the blood of bulls and goats could take away sins" (Heb. 10:4). Only Christ's sinless blood could do that. Only Jesus "washed us from our sins in His own blood" (Rev. 1:5). The Greek word translated *washed* means "to bathe the whole person." It is, indeed, a powerful word. It suggests a complete washing. When cleansed by Christ's blood, as I said before, sins are reckoned *as if they never happened*. This may be why some Christians appear much more joyful than others. They no longer carry the guilt and condemnation of their sin. They understand what the blood of Jesus has done to make them free.

The following story illustrates well the cleansing that comes through Jesus's blood.

> One night in a church service a young woman felt the tug of God at her heart. She responded to God's call and accepted Jesus as her Lord and Savior. The young woman had a very rough past involving alcohol, drugs, and prostitution. But the change in her was evident.
>
> As time went on, she became a faithful member of the church. She eventually became involved in the ministry, teaching young children. It was not very long until this faithful young woman caught the eye and heart of the pastor's son. The relationship grew, and they began to make wedding plans. This is when the problems began.
>
> You see, about half of the church did not think that a woman with a past such as hers was suitable for a pastor's son. The church began to argue and fight about the matter. So they decided to have a meeting. As the people made their arguments, tensions increased, and the meeting began to get completely out of hand. The young woman became very upset about all the things being brought up about her past. As she began to cry, the pastor's son stood to speak. He could not bear the pain it was causing his wife-to-be. So he said, "My fiancée's past is not what is on trial here. What you are questioning is the ability of the blood of Jesus to wash away sin. Today you have put the blood of Jesus on trial. So does it wash away sin or not?"
>
> The whole church began to weep as they realized that they had been slandering the blood of the Lord Jesus Christ. Too often, even as Christians, we bring up the past and use it as a weapon against our brothers and sisters. Forgiveness is a very foundational part of the gospel. If the blood of Jesus does not cleanse another person completely, then it cannot cleanse us completely. If that is the case, then we are all in a lot of trouble. What can

wash away my sins? Nothing but the blood of Jesus! End of case![3]

—ANONYMOUS

The blood of Jesus completely cleanses us of our sins and by so doing allows us to boldly enter God's presence. We read in the Book of Hebrews, "Therefore, brethren, having boldness to enter the Holiest by the blood of Jesus" (Heb. 10:19). Imagine that! A person can come with confidence, assurance, and even boldness into God's presence, knowing that he will be received because his sins no longer separate him from God. No longer do we have to feel God disapproves of us; that fear is now out of the way so that we can fellowship with our Creator.

STAYING FREE FROM SIN

We were never meant to continue to live in sin after receiving God's saving grace. But, unfortunately, while we are in this life, we are susceptible to sin. John assures us that the blood of Jesus is not good for only one cleansing but has the power to keep us clean: "If we walk in the light as He is in the light, we have fellowship with one another, and the blood of Jesus Christ His Son cleanses us from all sin" (1 John 1:7). And, "If we confess our sins, He is faithful and just to forgive us our sins and to cleanse us from all unrighteousness" (v. 9). Again John was not saying that a believer, now freed from sin, should continue practicing sin. There is a clear difference between "living" in sin and occasionally "falling" into it. There is a difference between "practicing" sin and being "troubled" by it.

Some believe that a person can be freed from sin in such a way that he or she will never sin again. The Bible does not teach the attainment of sinless perfection. Rather it teaches freedom from the "power" of sin, which means that a person is no longer "forced" to sin. "Sin shall not have dominion over you, for you are not under law but under grace" (Rom. 6:14). After you have been cleansed by the blood of Jesus, sin becomes a matter of choice. One can reject the power of the indwelling

Christ and choose to sin, or he can call upon the righteousness that is in Jesus and experience His help in overcoming sin. He is no longer obligated to do wrong by "the law of sin." (See Romans 7:14–25.)

Jesus is the solution. We read in 1 John 2:1–2, "My little children, these things I write to you, so that you may not sin. And if anyone sins, we have an Advocate with the Father, Jesus Christ the righteous. And He Himself is the propitiation for our sins, and not for ours only but also for the whole world."

Later we will look carefully at what it means to have "Christ in us." For now I want to continue to emphasize that the righteousness required of us is not administered or controlled by the Law, and it is not accomplished without God's help. The good news of the gospel is not only that Christ died for sinners but also that He came to take up residence in the life of a believer. This and only this is what makes real righteousness possible. The life of Christ in us gives the strength to do what we cannot do by ourselves. Of all the truths of God's Word, this is one of the most misunderstood and neglected. For some reason we gravitate to the Law or to works to make us righteous rather than to Christ, and in the process we miss God's grace and power.

When you are tempted, angry, fearful, neglected, discouraged, depressed, or plagued by whatever else is bugging your life, cry out to God for help. Just pray, "Father, manifest the grace, mercy, and power of Jesus in me right now. I need Your help." Or if you want to be a little less formal, you might want to pray like this, "Father, please do something in me right now because I'm about to explode! Help!" Either way He gets the point. Remember, "It is God who works in you both to will and to do for His good pleasure" (Phil. 2:13).

CALVARY

Before we close this chapter, I want to point out the significance of the cross of Christ, which stood on a hill called Calvary. One of the most significant events in history is Jesus's death on the cross. Without it mankind would be hopelessly lost. The cross remains a symbol of where Christ shed His blood to redeem us. Every Christian should often remember its importance and power. Volumes have been written on the subject, yet we have but scratched the surface of the significance of Calvary's cross. I want to make three observations here about the importance of the cross.

First, because of the blood shed on the cross, rebellion will never be an issue once the redeemed are with their Lord. It will never be a consideration in heaven regardless of continuing free will. Once the price of salvation is fully understood and the love shown at Calvary is fully comprehended, the redeemed will forever be awestruck lovers of the Christ who has "loved us and given Himself for us" (Eph. 5:2).

Second, the cross stands for life as well as death. This is where the eternal life of God, the very heart and mind of the universe, was displayed to the world, for in Jesus dwells "all the fullness of the Godhead bodily" (Col. 2:9).

And third, the measure of the work of Jesus on the cross must also be a measurable work in us. Paul wrote, "I have been crucified with Christ" (Gal. 2:20). And, "But God forbid that I should boast except in the cross of our Lord Jesus Christ, by whom the world has been crucified to me, and I to the world" (Gal. 6:14). Jesus Himself said, "And he who does not take his cross and follow after Me is not worthy of Me" (Matt. 10:38).

H. A. Maxwell Whyte writes, "When we consider the great load of sin and guilt which Jesus carried on Calvary, is it any wonder that He cried in agony of soul (not so much of body), 'My God, my God, why hast thou forsaken me?' (Psalm 22:1; Matthew 27:46). But why had the Father forsaken the Son? Because it is written that God cannot look upon sin (Habakkuk 1:13). When Jesus was bearing the sins of the world in His body on the cross, the Father could not look at His Son. Jesus had become sin for us (2 Corinthians 5:21)."[4]

CHAPTER 17

A Radical Substitution

*And they sang a new song, saying: "You are worthy
to take the scroll, and to open its seals; for You were
slain, and have redeemed us to God by Your blood out
of every tribe and tongue and people and nation."*

—Revelation 5:9

MANY PEOPLE WRESTLE from time to time with the way
God appears to deal with humanity. In some cases,
especially in the Old Testament, He seems to be overwhelmingly dictatorial, even heartless. Some people think He created
a world that He really doesn't much like, mostly because people
refuse to follow His rules. To them He seems to be saying,
"Obey Me or else, because I'm really upset and I'm tired of
dealing with all of this stuff on earth!"

You don't have to be treated badly as a child to perceive God
in this manner. There are parts of Scripture that seem to support this notion, especially when taken out of context. Without
a careful reading of the Old Testament and comparing it to the
New, it's easy to pick up negative ideas concerning God's character. On top of that, one of the chief tactics of the enemy of
our souls is to distort our perception of God in order to destroy
any potential relationship with Him.

Perception is a major part of how we relate to others and
even to God. As an example, how do you perceive this statement? "But if you do not obey Me, and do not observe all these
commandments, and if you despise My statutes, or if your soul
abhors My judgments, so that you do not perform all My commandments, but break My covenant, I also will do this to you:

I will even appoint terror over you, wasting disease and fever which shall consume the eyes and cause sorrow of heart. And you shall sow your seed in vain, for your enemies shall eat it" (Lev. 26:14–16).

You may know God well enough to understand that He is full of compassion and doesn't make irrational, heartless statements. You may realize that He doesn't get angry and fly into a rage when someone does something He doesn't like. You may also understand that when you filter this statement in Leviticus through other passages of Scripture and your own personal walk with God, you realize that He knows what He is doing and saying, that it is without error, and that He is very much a "good" God.

David declared, "The statues of the Lord are right, rejoicing the heart; the commandment of the Lord is pure, enlightening the eyes; the fear of the Lord is clean, enduring forever; the judgments of the Lord are true and righteous altogether" (Ps. 19:8–9). But if you haven't really spent time with God through prayer and gotten to know Him by studying His Word, then you may perceive this statement from Leviticus as graceless, mean, and indifferent.

Most of God's anger comes as a result of broken covenants. You can almost hear Him say, "I thought we had an agreement. What do you mean you are no longer interested in having a relationship with Me?"

God is not the only one who takes violating an agreement seriously. The laws of a land usually safeguard citizens against actions that are injurious to others. Lawbreakers are required to pay for their wrongdoing. They may be sorry and that may help them get a lighter sentence, but if they break the law, there is going to be a reckoning. It should come as no surprise that God operates in a similar manner. If you break one of His laws, there is a penalty. And because God writes His covenants in blood, that penalty may be blood.

Sometimes society deals casually with certain lawbreakers.

Grace is wonderful, but sometimes leniency can do more harm than good. The person who has been arrested numerous times for driving drunk or for selling drugs or for stealing needs someone to say, "That's enough." God too won't keep letting us wreak havoc on ourselves and others with our sinful ways. Even if He stays His anger for a while, a day of reckoning will come. And when it comes to sin, the Bible is clear: "Without shedding of blood there is no remission [forgiveness]" (Heb. 9:22).

In God's eyes punishment is warranted when someone harms someone else. This is the point of Jesus's remarks that all the Law and the Prophets hang on two commandments: to love God and to love others (Matt. 22:39–40). That may sound simplistic, but failure to keep these two commandments results in the kind of world we live in today, one filled with violence and heartache. There is a penalty for failing to love (respect, honor, regard, and value), and that price must be paid in blood. This means someone has to die. If this sounds capricious, always keep in mind what sin has done to our world.

RECONCILED TO THE FATHER

If God had not been gracious to provide a sacrifice for our sins in Jesus's blood, there would be no reconciliation. As I've said before, forgiveness of sin is not arbitrary. God can't say, "OK, now that you are sorry, I will forget what you have done." God releases us from our sin debt only after full payment for the debt has been rendered. And that payment is made only with blood. This is why, again, we read, "Without the shedding of blood there is no remission [forgiveness]" (Heb. 9:22). When Jesus's blood goes to work to atone for our sins, two things happen. First, His blood cancels the debt created by offenses against God and man. And because the debt is canceled, we no longer have to be bound by the guilt and shame of those sins.[1] Second, His blood destroys the power of sin, the very thing that was passed to us from Adam that causes us to do sinful things.

The provisions God made to reconcile us to Himself are wonderful, but consider for a moment what life would be like without it. That, in essence, is what hell is all about. It is the choice one makes when he decides to reject God's way of reconciliation. Hell was never designed for mankind. It was made for the devil and his angels (Matt. 25:41). In a very real sense God is going to throw sin into hell, and anyone holding on to it will go right along with it.

Sin literally results in eternal separation from God. Some may have a problem with God responding to sin in this manner, but they probably have little problem separating themselves from criminals in this life. Simply put, God doesn't want to be around people who insist on rebelling against His laws any more than we want to be around people who insist on breaking man's laws. Furthermore, we are no less of a mind to require them to pay for their misconduct in a manner commensurate to the wrongdoing.

The exception, again, is that even in this life there is a tendency to show mercy when the offender shows remorse. But typically mercy isn't granted until the offended party is appeased. The general attitude is that when a wrong is committed, someone must pay. In some cases it doesn't matter who pays just as long as the offended is satisfied. Such is the case in the court of heaven. The matter will not be dropped until the offended is content. And God is deeply offended when His creation is abused.

It is here that, again, we trace the message of substitution. Remember that if someone were willing to become a substitute and pay for someone else's sin, that person would have to be blameless, owing no debt himself. If such a person could be found, a lot of fast-talking would be needed to convince him to pay the price for someone else's sin. But, again, it would be impossible to find such a person because no one is without sin. This is why we needed Jesus and why He had to be born of a virgin. Only through a miraculous conception could a person be born without sin and thereby be an eligible substitute for others.

In the words of the apostle Paul, Jesus *"gave Himself for our sins*, that he might deliver us from this present evil age" (Gal. 1:4, emphasis added). Notice the words "gave Himself." In other words, He became our substitute. Other passages of Scripture make the same point: "I have been crucified with Christ; it is no longer I who live, but Christ lives in me; and the life which I now live in the flesh I live by faith in the Son of God, *who loved me and gave Himself for me*" (Gal. 2:20, emphasis added). And, "Looking for the blessed hope and glorious appearing of our great God and Savior Jesus Christ, *who gave Himself for us*, that He might redeem us from every lawless deed and purify for Himself *His* own special people, zealous for good works" (Titus 2:13–14, emphasis added).

It is vitally important that we understand that Jesus "gave Himself" by shedding His blood at Calvary. And only by His blood do we find forgiveness for our sins.

Substitution is also seen in 2 Corinthians 5:21: "For He made Him who knew no sin to be sin for us, that we might become the righteousness of God in Him." Discussing substitution, Bible scholar Leon Morris wrote, "When the New Testament speaks of redemption, then, unless our linguistics are at fault, it means that Christ has paid the price of our redemption. To the extent that the price paid must be adequate for the purchase in question this indicates an equivalence, a substitution."[2]

And New Testament scholar Kenneth Wuest had this to say about substitution: "The problem of how a just God could require that justice be satisfied in the case of the human breaking His law, and mercy be offered the evil doer, was solved by the substitutionary atonement. The Judge in this case steps down from His judgment throne to take upon Himself the guilt and penalty of the sinner. In this way justice was satisfied, His government maintained, and the flood gates of mercy opened, resulting in the righteous bestowal of salvation."[3]

Not only was Jesus the substitute in paying for our sins this side of the cross, but His death also reached back to provide full payment for the sins of those on the other side of the cross as well. We look back to the cross for our redemption, and the saints in the Old Testament looked "forward" to it. Animal sacrifices in the Old Testament were substitutes for the real substitute and would no longer be needed once the final offering for sin was made. The blood of bulls and goats was insufficient to take care of sin. In the Old Testament it sufficed only until the final sacrifice (our substitute) would come. "For it is not possible that the blood of bulls and goats could take away sins" (Heb. 10:4).

The writer of Hebrews went on to say: "We have been sanctified through the offering of the body of Jesus Christ once *for all*. And every priest stands ministering daily and offering repeatedly the same sacrifices, which can never take away sins. But this Man, after He had offered one sacrifice for sins forever, sat down at the right hand of God, from that time waiting till His enemies are made His footstool. For by one offering He has perfected forever those who are being sanctified. But the Holy Spirit also witnesses to us; for after He had said before, *'This is the covenant that I will make with them after those days, says the LORD: I will put My laws into their hearts, and in their minds I will write them,'* then He adds, *'Their sins and their lawless deeds I will remember no more.'* Now where there is remission of these, there is no longer an offering for sin" (vv. 10–18, emphasis added).

Bible teacher Charles Pfeiffer explains the substitutionary work of Jesus this way: "The sacrifice of Christ gives the believer a position before God, so that we may say that he is justified. It provides a righteousness which is imputed to the believer, and it also imparts a power to the believer so that 'dead works' are purged away. The works of the spiritually dead man are 'dead works,' but the newborn Christian now has a divine power whereby he is enabled 'to serve the living God.' In his own strength, the believer is no more able to serve God than the sinner was able to save himself. All of the graces which the Spirit bestows on us find their basis in the work of Christ. It is because the blood was shed that we can now, depending on the Spirit, serve God."[4]

NEW LIFE IN CHRIST

It was not the life of Christ before His death that provided cleansing from sin, but His blood as the result of His death.[5] Now, after His death, Christ's resurrected life instills new life into the believer. Again, Paul preached "Christ in you, the hope of glory" (Col. 1:27). God's Spirit, when invited to enter the human heart, creates a holiness and righteousness not attainable by human effort—"Not by works of righteousness which we have done, but according to His mercy He saved us, through the washing of regeneration and renewing of the Holy Spirit" (Titus 3:5).

Paul's saying "not by works of righteousness" makes it clear that God is not looking for us to deal with sin on our own. Religions that stress following strict rules as a means of attaining salvation cannot possibly offer mankind any hope for dealing with sin.

CHAPTER 18

Communion: Celebrating the New Covenant

For as often as you eat this bread and drink this cup,
you proclaim the Lord's death till He comes.

—1 Corinthians 11:26

In the Old Testament the Passover observance served as a reminder of how God delivered the children of Israel from slavery in Egypt. Passover also reminded them of the need for blood to ratify an agreement with God. In other words, Passover was as a memorial acknowledging that the people were in blood covenant with their Creator. The blood the Israelites put on the lintel (the support beam above the door) and on the doorposts of the house was the sign of the agreement. They could look at it and remember that they made an agreement with God. In judging Egypt, God agreed to pass over His own people if they would again accept the covenant with Him. Covenanting with God provided Israel with both blessing and protection.

In the New Testament a similar memorial is observed. It's called Communion, and it corresponds to the Passover memorial in the Old Testament. Jesus wanted His followers to always remember that they were in covenant with Him, which is why He initiated Communion with the Lord's Supper.

The apostle Paul explained Communion this way: "The cup of blessing which we bless, is it not the communion of the blood of Christ? The bread which we break, is it not the communion of the body of Christ?" (1 Cor. 10:16). These are powerful words. Notice that the "cup" is the "communion of the blood." In other words, it represents the commingling of blood and the transfer of the rights and privileges of one person to another. This is blood covenant.

Communion is a reminder of our covenant relationship with God through Christ. It is no accident that Jesus used the word *remembrance* twice when He introduced the ordinance. "And when He had given thanks, He broke it and said, 'Take, eat; this is My body which is broken for you; do this in *remembrance* of Me.' In the same manner He also took the cup after supper, saying, 'This cup is the new covenant in My blood. This do, as often as you drink it, in *remembrance* of Me.'" (1 Cor. 11:24–25, emphasis added).

Every time we eat the bread and drink the Communion cup, we should realize four things:

1. Christ's body has been broken for us (represented by the broken bread). This is the most remarkable act of love (1 Cor. 11:24).

2. We are in blood covenant with God (represented by the juice of the grape) and have moved from the kingdom of darkness to the kingdom of light (John 5:24).

3. Jesus has paid the price of broken covenants with His own blood; in other words, He is our substitute (Gal. 1:4).

4. God's presence is at the table when we partake (Matt. 18:20).

Communion is observed[1] in different ways depending upon custom and tradition.[2] It is typically a time of contemplation and reflection about the need for remorse and repentance for sin. Without question it should always be observed with reverence and respect. But it also should be a time of rejoicing. It would be safe to say that some Christians don't really look forward to Communion. They have been taught to honor its sacredness, but they have not been shown how to celebrate it. In some cases celebrating Communion is profoundly discouraged, as leaders try instead to cause people to feel conviction by urging them to "look at the cross and see Jesus hanging there." And then to "realize you put Him there."

Certainly our sin is responsible for the suffering Christ endured. But Jesus Himself said He did not come into the world to condemn the world (John 3:17). If Jesus were to speak to the matter today, He might say something to the effect of, "Yes, I hung on the cross and suffered and died there for you. But I didn't do it to make you feel worse; I did it to make you feel better. In fact, I did it, in part, because there was no other way that you would believe I love you unless I did something that drastic. Oh, and by the way, I'm not hanging there anymore. I'm seated at the right hand of the Father, and things here are just fine."

It used to be that when I came to church and saw the Communion table set, I felt a sinking feeling deep inside. I don't think I dreaded Communion, but it's probably safe to say that I wasn't very fond of it. I'm not sure why this happened, but it no doubt had something to do with teachings I'd heard that suggested this was a time to confront my sin. It also may have had to do with the fear generated by the teaching that I must not participate in Communion unworthily or something bad would happen to me.

The caution that we are not to participate in Communion haphazardly is appropriate. This admonition came straight from the Bible: "But let a man examine himself, and so let him eat of the bread and drink of the cup. For he who eats and drinks in an unworthy manner eats and drinks judgment to himself, not discerning the Lord's body" (1 Cor. 11:28–29). Communion is a serious moment, and those who do not understand covenant relationship with God or who are living in sin need to understand we are at God's table.

Nevertheless, the atmosphere for Communion is not to be somber and grave. This is not a time to invoke fear. We can be serious without being fearful or melancholy. Certainly this is a good time to deal with any sin that hasn't already been addressed, keeping in mind that it can be cleansed by Jesus's blood through confession and repentance at any time (1 John 1:9). But it is also a time to celebrate with Jesus. It is a time to rejoice and be glad. God wants all who put their trust in Him to rejoice and be joyful in Him (Ps. 5:11).

Everything God does has purpose. Most of what He does with His people has to do with bringing restoration, reconciliation, fellowship, holiness, and hope. He's far less interested in form and fancy than some may think. Communion then is to involve not only remembrance and heart searching, but also—and especially—celebration. The joy of what Christ did must never be lost in mere form, even when the form is representative of people trying to obey God's Word. To let Communion get lost in the rigors of ritual is to lose its meaning, its beauty, and especially its power. We cannot forget that the elements are not the only things at the Communion table; God's presence is there as well. In this wonderful celebration of our reconciliation with God, His Spirit surrounds the table—and us, His people. That alone is reason to rejoice.

CHAPTER 19

Blessing and Power
Through Jesus's Blood

The cup of blessing which we bless, is it not the communion
of the blood of Christ? The bread which we break,
is it not the communion of the body of Christ?

—1 Corinthians 10:16

PERHAPS ONLY IN eternity will we truly realize how blessed we are by God. It is easy to take for granted "everyday" blessings such as warm clothes, good food, and wonderful friends. These things don't just "happen." Behind the scenes God is making sure that everything works to our benefit (Rom. 8:28). But as wonderful as it is to have life, health, and strength, the real blessing is the manifestation of God's presence to His people. This became available to anyone who desired it beginning when Jesus met with His disciples in the Upper Room and took the cup and used its contents to make a new covenant with mankind (1 Cor. 11:25).

The "blood of the grape" was used in place of real blood to establish the agreement. No doubt the disciples at the table with Jesus understood what a blood covenant was. They were Jews and certainly familiar with the old covenant. Very possibly they had seen blood covenants made before. So when Jesus was preparing to make the covenant, all He needed was blood. But as we have seen, instead of using His own blood to mingle with that of the disciples, He used substitutionary blood, the blood of the grape.

Why did Jesus use substitutionary blood in making the agreement? It is possible that His sinless blood could not be mingled directly with sin-tainted human blood. The idea is worthy of exploration, but there may be a better explanation. It may be that Jesus knew that if His own blood touched the blood of the disciples, some would conclude that the miraculous signs they performed were due to the fact that their blood had been mingled with Jesus's. Had this happened, Satan could have easily suggested, "Only the disciples who walked with Jesus had the power of Jesus, a power that was conveyed on them when their blood touched His blood. Therefore, miracles are not for today because nobody today has had their blood touch the blood of Jesus." But because Jesus used substitutionary blood, such claims could not be made.

The entire church has been "deputized," if you will, to perform miracles. Jesus said, "Most assuredly, I say to you, he who believes in Me, the works that I do he will do also; and greater works than these he will do, because I go to My Father" (John 14:12). Jesus did not say, "He whose blood has touched mine" can perform these greater works. He said, "He who believes in Me." Every generation of faithful Christians possesses the power to "trample on serpents and scorpions" and has been given authority "over all the power of the enemy" (Luke 10:19).

In addition, Jesus may have chosen not to mingle His actual blood with that of the disciples so future generations wouldn't think blood was still needed to make covenants, resulting in a continuation of animal sacrifices. Modern worship would have taken a far different form if Jesus had established the new covenant in any way other than the way He did.

Because of the shed blood of Christ believers now have authority as Christ's representatives here on earth (Luke 10:19). I close this chapter by noting a few rights and responsibilities concerning the authority Christ has given His church:

- *Jesus has all power both in heaven and on earth.*
  "And Jesus came and spoke to them, saying, 'All authority has been given to Me in heaven and on earth'" (Matt. 28:18). We must not assume that

the power we receive through Jesus is mystical
or magical or in some way needs to be conjured
up. It is to be used in the same manner Jesus
used it—calmly but with authority. We are to be
direct but not overpowering.

Jesus was always in control both of the situation and Himself. He never let things get out
of hand. Nor did He take credit for what had
happened (miracles, healings, the dead raised,
demons cast out). He always passed the credit to
the Father.

- *The power needed for spiritual warfare comes only
from and through Jesus.* "I am the vine, you are
the branches. He who abides in Me, and I in
him, bears much fruit; for without Me you
can do nothing" (John 15:5). It is incorrect to
think that when Jesus gave us power, He gave
it unconditionally—that we could use it at any
time and in any circumstance we wanted. He
did not send us out as rulers but as ambassadors.
Ambassadors take their orders from someone
higher; they act on behalf of someone else. This
is one reason that if we are to represent Christ,
we must know what He is saying. And that
comes through studying the Word and prayer.

- *We are not to rejoice in the power to cast out
demons.* "Nevertheless do not rejoice in this, that
the spirits are subject to you, but rather rejoice
because your names are written in heaven" (Luke
10:20). There are specific reasons we are not to
get excited and celebrate when demons are cast
out. First is the tendency toward pride when
we see God's power working through us. In a
similar way pride draws attention to witch doctors and palm readers. In the end they rejoice

over the fame and fortune that has come their way. This results in control, and control of people ruins a person's ability to love them, thus the second law of God is broken. Second, pride opens doors to demon spirits. Great ministries have come undone when arrogance entered the heart of the leader. Satan himself was cast from heaven because of pride and a desire for control that wasn't legitimate (Isa. 14:12–14).

- *We can get into trouble if God isn't directing us into battle.* "Then some of the itinerant Jewish exorcists took it upon themselves to call the name of the Lord Jesus over those who had evil spirits, saying, 'We exorcise you by the Jesus whom Paul preaches.' Also there were seven sons of Sceva, a Jewish chief priest, who did so. And the evil spirit answered and said, 'Jesus I know, and Paul I know; but who are you?' Then the man in whom the evil spirit was leaped on them, overpowered them, and prevailed against them, so that they fled out of that house naked and wounded" (Acts 19:13–16). Satan and his demons recognize Jesus's authority. Anyone who tries to mimic it, consciously or unconsciously, not only opens himself to God's discipline but also to attacks by demons as well. The sons of Sceva are case in point.

CHAPTER 20

Nobody Can Touch the Baby

*Being justified freely by His grace through
the redemption that is in Christ Jesus.*

—ROMANS 3:24

IN PREVIOUS CHAPTERS we've discovered the power of substitution. We've seen it at work in *making* a covenant. Let's
look at it at work once again when the covenant is broken.

A powerful story concerning substitution, especially as it
relates to one person giving his life for another, comes from
the lives of missionaries John and Betty Stam and their baby
daughter, Helen. John and Betty met at Moody Bible Institute
in Chicago, Illinois. Their love for each other led to marriage,
and their love for God drew them to China where Betty had
grown up in the home of missionary parents.

Their work was to be in Tsingteh in China's southern Anhwei
Province. A short time after arriving in the early 1930s, a
Communist uprising in a neighboring province resulted in the
invasion of their community. John and Betty were arrested and
accused of crimes against the Chinese people. Eventually they
were sentenced to death.

They were to be marched twelve miles to nearby Miaosheo.
While preparing for the journey, their newborn baby, Helen,
began to cry. One of the soldiers suggested killing her then
and there to spare them any trouble while traveling. At that
point an elderly Chinese farmer stepped forward proclaiming
the innocence of the child.

"She's done nothing worthy of death," he said.

"Then it's your life for hers!" the soldiers shouted.

The farmer agreed to their horrible terms, and soon after he was killed. Someone had substituted his life for another. As a result, baby Helen's life was spared.

Certainly Helen and her parents were judged wrongly. Neither John nor Betty had in any way wronged the Chinese people. Regardless, since Helen belonged to parents who were considered guilty, she too was being sentenced to death. It wasn't until her "substitute" came forward that she was allowed to live. Perhaps these men were acquainted with the age-old idea that once the price of an offense was paid, the guilty party was set free, as if she had done no wrong. After that nobody touched the baby.

In like manner Jesus stepped forward to take the place of all who had offended God's laws. He became their substitute. God was willing to pay the price for every evil deed ever committed by humanity. "But now, once at the end of the ages, He has appeared to put away sin by the sacrifice of Himself. . . . So Christ was offered once to bear the sins of many" (Heb. 9:26, 28).

The Stams were soon taken from the abandoned mansion in which they were held after arriving in Miaosheo and compelled to disrobe to their underwear. They were then marched through the village and out to a place called Eagle Hill. There John was ordered to his knees. The swiftness of the executioner's sword separated his head from his body as Betty looked on. Moments later she too entered the presence of Jesus with her husband. While this was happening, Helen lay in a room in a nearby house. With certainty we can say that God was watching over her, but she still needed to be physically rescued. Evangelist Lo, a Christian associate of the Stams, found her and smuggled her out of the town, where eventually she was returned to her grandparents in America. Helen's life was spared because of substitution. The death of another person, that old farmer, resulted in her freedom.[1]

Few real-life stories carry the remarkable resemblance to the substitutionary death of Jesus as does this one. An elderly

Chinese Christian man took Helen's place. Jesus took our place. Now nobody can touch the baby, and we are the baby! I'm the baby, and so are you if you have asked Christ to bring you into covenant relationship with Him. Now when Satan's demons come to accuse, harass, belittle, or condemn, we can tell them, "Nobody can touch the baby. Oh, and by the way, I'm the baby!"

GOD KNOWS WHAT HE IS DOING

Many people struggle to understand why God allowed the lives of such a precious young couple to be taken so violently. They worked so hard to get to the mission field only to serve for a short time and die tragically, leaving their baby daughter without her parents. Only God can truly answer those heart-rending questions. But sometimes after time has passed, He allows us to glimpse the good He works through these tragic situations. Or to put it another way, we are allowed to see what the tree looks like after its seed has fallen into the ground and died.

In the case of the Stams there is no way to know how many people responded to a call to missions upon hearing the story of their martyrdom. Plus, in 1935 the ministry the Stams were associated with, the China Inland Mission, received sizable donations, far more than in previous years. John and Betty's biography eventually went through nine printings. A new vision for missions touched the hearts of many people wherever the Stams' story was told.

Today China is experiencing a powerful move of God. Large numbers of people are finding Christ. John and Betty still remain a part of this great mission's movement to reach the lost. Their story of Calvary's love continues to be told.

Nobody relishes pain. Who gets up in the morning saying, "This is going to be another wonderful, painful day"? On the contrary, we do everything we know to do to avoid suffering and sorrow. But God warns us that pain and suffering will be a part of our lives while we are here on earth. Scripture says, "Beloved, do not think it strange concerning the fiery trial which is to try you, as though some strange thing happened to you; but rejoice to the extent that you partake of Christ's sufferings, that when His glory is revealed, you may also be glad with exceeding joy" (1 Pet. 4:12–13).

Once while in a meeting my friend was seated next to a woman who was rejoicing that she would not have to go through the Tribulation.[2] My friend couldn't resist pursuing the subject, noting that in much of our world there are people going through difficulty that would match whatever suffering she felt might occur in the days ahead. The woman responded that she could not bear to suffer the way she believed many will have to in the future. She even indicated that she was unwilling to serve God if that were her fate. Jim simply responded, "That's the whole point," because a Christian is called to follow Christ, even when it's uncomfortable.

CHAPTER 21

God's Purpose in Covenant Making

Therefore, if anyone is in Christ, he is a new creation; old things have passed away; behold, all things have become new.

—2 Corinthians 5:17

THERE APPEARS TO be at least two reasons God established a covenant as part of His redemption plan. First is for fellowship and restoration. We, the "new creation" (2 Cor. 5:17), are to be reestablished in the image and likeness of Jesus and brought back into relationship with God. His desire is to restore what was lost through sin. But, again, no amount of change is possible until a person aligns himself or herself with God through Jesus. This is the only way to be made right before God. Salvation comes only through a relationship with God through Jesus (Acts 4:12). When we align with God and allow Him to lead, we enter the restoration process.

Every moment we walk in the kingdom of light brings change. Make no mistake; transformation of character happens bit by bit and piece by piece. "But we all, with unveiled face, beholding as in a mirror the glory of the Lord, are being transformed into the same image *from glory to glory*, just as by the Spirit of the Lord" (2 Cor. 3:18, emphasis added). We don't become mature in Christ overnight. We are people in process. Today's glorious change will not be as bright as tomorrow's. And the day after will be even brighter. The change is sometimes slow, and we may not readily see what God is doing in us. But we can rest assured that He is always working in us (Phil. 2:13). We must not become discouraged with the process.

The second reason God wanted to establish a covenant relationship with mankind was to create a lineage into which Jesus could be born. Two lineages are given for Jesus, one in the Book of Matthew and the other in the Book of Luke. Both show that Joseph's and Mary's ancestry could be traced back to Abraham with whom God established the covenant of promise. This is extremely important in order to show that Jesus was part of God's covenant people. When God promised a "Seed" (Gen. 3:15) who would deal with both sin and Satan, He promised to provide that seed through Abraham. These lineages show that.

It took God several thousand years of working in mankind to set an appropriate stage on which to introduce His Son. And "when the fullness of the time had come, God sent forth His Son, born of a woman, born under the law" (Gal. 4:4). The virgin birth cannot be minimized. Without the sinless nature of Jesus we would have no gospel and no salvation. As another note: while neither Joseph nor Mary tainted Jesus's sinless blood with their own, they did provide a proper atmosphere into which He could be born and grow. Mary was known for her purity and Joseph for his integrity. If pagan parents had raised Jesus, or adulterers or thieves, it would be difficult to believe in His goodness.[1]

WHERE IT ALL ENDS

God is in the process of rescuing this world. Once He has accomplished His plan, He will restructure both heaven and earth: "Now I saw a new heaven and a new earth, for the first heaven and the first earth had passed away. Also there was no more sea" (Rev. 21:1). What we currently see as reality will soon disappear. This has been the message and hope of the church for nearly two thousand years—in reality for all of human existence. And yet some Christians don't talk much of their hope. You don't hear them speak often about the return of Jesus. Sadly this leaves a vacuum in the world that is being filled by one apocalyptic theory after another. People seem to realize that we are on a collision course with eternity, and they talk about the dawning of a new age. They realize that this world is doomed in its present condition and that things must change, but there is only one plan of redemption. It can't be found in the Mayan calendar or through extraterrestrials. Our hope is not in exploring new planets or even in rejuvenating this one. Our hope for redemption comes only through Christ. Jesus is coming again. The Bible is quite clear on this fact, as the following verses attest.

> Assuredly, I say to you, there are some standing here who shall not taste death till they see the Son of Man coming in His kingdom.
>
> —MATTHEW 16:28

> Now as He sat on the Mount of Olives, the disciples came to Him privately, saying, "Tell us, when will these things be? And what will be the sign of Your coming, and of the end of the age?"
>
> —MATTHEW 24:3

> And this gospel of the kingdom will be preached in all the world as a witness to all the nations, and then the end will come.
>
> —MATTHEW 24:14

> For as the lightning comes from the east and flashes to the west, so also will the coming of the Son of Man be.
>
> —MATTHEW 24:27

> Then the sign of the Son of Man will appear in heaven, and then all the tribes of the earth will mourn, and they will see the Son of Man coming on the clouds of heaven with power and great glory.
>
> —MATTHEW 24:30

> But as the days of Noah were, so also will the coming of the Son of Man be. For as in the days before the flood, they were eating and drinking, marrying and giving in marriage, until the day that Noah entered the ark, and

did not know until the flood came and took them all away, so also will the coming of the Son of Man be.

—MATTHEW 24:37–39

Watch therefore, for you do not know what hour your Lord is coming.

—MATTHEW 24:42

Therefore you also be ready, for the Son of Man is coming at an hour you do not expect.

—MATTHEW 24:44

But if that evil servant says in his heart, "My master is delaying his coming," and begins to beat his fellow servants, and to eat and drink with the drunkards, the master of that servant will come on a day when he is not looking for him and at an hour that he is not aware of, and will cut him in two and appoint him his portion with the hypocrites. There shall be weeping and gnashing of teeth.

—MATTHEW 24:48–51

Watch therefore, for you know neither the day nor the hour in which the Son of Man is coming.

—MATTHEW 25:13

Jesus said to him, "It is as you said. Nevertheless, I say to you, hereafter you will see the Son of Man sitting at the right hand of the Power, and coming on the clouds of heaven."

—MATTHEW 26:64

So you see the question for us is not whether He will return and bring His kingdom but whether we will accept His invitation to enter into covenant with Him and make ourselves ready.

CHAPTER 22

The Benefits of Covenant

*And they sang a new song, saying: "You are worthy to take
the scroll, and to open its seals; for You were slain, and
have redeemed us to God by Your blood out of every tribe
and tongue and people and nation, and have made us kings
and priests to our God; and we shall reign on the earth."*

—Revelation 5:9–10

SOME PREACHERS CLAIM that Christians have no rights.
Usually they are trying to make the point that Christians
don't have the right to live their lives anyway they please (1 Cor.
6:19). There is a certain amount of truth in this teaching, but
there's also just enough error to create confusion and in the
process damage individuals' spiritual lives. It is true that people
in covenant with God give up all rights to selfish ambitions and
to doing things their own way. But Christianity isn't meant to
make people into mindless, lifeless, animated robots with no
ability or freedom to choose.

God's people can claim many benefits, namely God's protection and blessings. The Bible says, "Then your light shall break
forth like the morning, your healing shall spring forth speedily,
and your righteousness shall go before you; *the glory of the LORD
shall be your rear guard*" (Isa. 58:8, emphasis added). So as you
can see, God has even promised to protect our backside.

When I was a young boy, a friend became angry and wanted
to do me bodily harm. I retreated to a wooden platform built
high up in some old oak trees. It was a place my friend and I
played together. Earlier it had been stocked with empty bev-
erage cans (the heavy ones, unlike the aluminum ones today) as

ammunition against enemies (we didn't really have any, at least I didn't until my friend became angry).

Up the ladder he came with fire in his eyes. I think he was yelling something to the effect that when he got his hands on me, he was going to kill me. I resorted to the cans and proceeded to bounce them off his head from above. I'm not suggesting he had a hard head, but the cans weren't working. In fact, they seemed to make the fire in him grow more intense. The rest of the story is one of those "just in the nick of time" tales. My mom evidently saw or heard the commotion and ran to the back door of our house and proceeded to yell at my friend. Thank God for Mom because he didn't get me.

And thank God for Daddy (Abba) God because He's not going to let the devil and his demons harm us either. "'No weapon formed against you shall prosper, and every tongue which rises against you in judgment you shall condemn. This is the heritage of the servants of the LORD, and their righteousness is from Me,' says the LORD" (Isa. 54:17).

My friend recognized my mother and her relationship to me as my protector. Satan's demons certainly recognize God, but they may fail to acknowledge our relationship with Him unless we mention it. Keep in mind that a believer's relationship with God has been established on the basis of covenant, and God actually keeps that relationship with Him as a matter of record by putting our names in His Book of Life (Phil. 4:3). So the next time you feel hassled by an ugly thought that says, "You're not saved," when in fact you have received Christ and are trying to live for Him, simply tell the harassing spirit, "Go check the record. I'm in covenant relationship with Jesus. I have rights, and one of those rights is freedom from you. Yeah, I was guilty of sin, but someone settled my account. Go check with Him."

In addition to protecting us, God also agrees to bless us. The real blessings He would like to give are yet to come (namely the joy of spending an eternity with Him), but while we are on this earth, He blesses us with His presence, His joy, His peace, material things, friends, health, and safety.

God blesses us not merely out of obligation to hold up His end of the covenant. He delights in blessing us, and as part of His willingness to bless, He also invites us to ask for things. "Ask, and it will be given to you; seek, and you will find; knock, and it will be opened to you. For everyone who asks receives, and he who seeks finds, and to him who knocks it will be opened" (Matt. 7:7–8). Some ministers teach that God's people should possess an abundance of material things—fancy cars, big homes, expensive clothes, and a variety of other "stuff." In a way this is true. But it is also misleading. Like any good Father, God wants to give nice things to His children. The Bible says, "Every good gift and every perfect gift is from above, and comes down from the Father of lights, with whom there is no variation or shadow of turning" (James 1:17). At the same time God knows some things aren't good for us right now. His will is that we set our affection—or our desire—on eternal things (Col. 3:2). When we seek Him first, He gives us all we need.

GETTING THE EARTH BACK

In order to understand redemption, it is important to understand why this world is in its current condition. In the Book of Genesis we see that God gave Adam dominion over the planet. But Adam through his disobedience to God forfeited that dominion to Satan. Adam's disobedience allowed the enemy to usurp control of the place God, in essence, loaned to Adam to rule. Adam ruled this world with God's help for a period of time. Then when Adam essentially said, "I'd like to try some things on my own," sin entered the world, and it began to spin out of his control. In the process Satan moved in and took the rulership away from Adam.

Jesus is in the process of getting that rulership back. Jesus said, "Now is the judgment of this world; now the ruler [Satan] of this world will be cast out" (John 12:31). The reason Jesus doesn't arbitrarily step in and claim possession now has to do with jurisprudence. This rulership issue is a legal matter, and God is settling the whole thing lawfully. Through Christ's blood God is legally dealing with Adam's crime.

For God to put the earth back into mankind's hands people would have to be free from sin and from Satan's influence. The Bible says we will once again "reign on the earth" (Rev. 5:10). Although Satan is the ruler of earth today (Luke 4:6; 1 John 5:19), humanity will again take control of it with Christ sometime in the future. But all of this happens only because of the legal developments resulting from Christ's death on the cross through which the Father granted freedom from the enemy's influence and control. As the apostle Paul put it, "He has delivered us from the power of darkness and conveyed us into the kingdom of the Son of His love" (Col. 1:13).

Because of this, to put it simply, Satan and his demons can't touch a Christian unless God permits it: "We know that whoever is born of God does not sin; but he who has been born of God keeps himself, and the wicked one does not touch him" (1 John 5:18). This, of course, is true only so long as a person is found abiding in covenant relationship with God and living in accordance with the godly principles of the new kingdom, including the principle of putting on the whole armor of God (Eph. 6:11). It is possible, by sinful living, to open doors to the enemy and to experience satanic attacks as a result (though, to be clear, not all satanic attacks are caused by doors we open to the enemy through disobedience). This is why we must protect ourselves by living righteously and by putting on the whole armor of God (vv. 10–17) "that [we] may be able to withstand in the evil day" (v. 13).

Christ has authority over Satan both because He is God and because as a man He was sinless. Those in covenant relationship with God have power over the enemy because He has taken away their sin and then "deputized" them to do the very works that He did (John 14:12). This deputized power is clearly revealed in the statement "Behold, I give you the authority to trample on serpents and scorpions [demons], and over all the power of the enemy" (Luke 10:19). It may seem that we struggle against individuals or circumstances, but the Bible makes it clear that the real battle for a Christian is a spiritual one—"For we do not wrestle against flesh and blood, but against principalities, against powers, against the rulers of the darkness of this age, against spiritual hosts of wickedness in the heavenly places" (Eph. 6:12).

The power we have over the enemy is based solely on the fact that we have God's abiding presence in us. We overcome the enemy "because He who is in [us] is greater than he who is in the world" (1 John 4:4).

LEGALLY FREE FROM SIN

As long as a person walks in darkness, he is bound to both sin and Satan and cannot fight the good fight of faith (2 Tim. 4:7). By obtaining liberty through the blood of Jesus, a person is able to have his bondage reversed and to begin to live in freedom. Christ's death and resurrection legally free the sinner from the power of sin and the dictates of the enemy. "Knowing this, that our old man was crucified with Him, that the body of sin might be done away with, that we should no longer be slaves of sin. For he who has died has been *freed from sin*. Now if we died with Christ, we believe that we shall also live with Him" (Rom. 6:6–8, emphasis added).

The apostle Paul goes on to say, "For sin shall not have dominion over you, for you are not under law but under grace" (v. 14). Moving from the kingdom of darkness to the kingdom of light through the new covenant legally changes the administration over us as well as the administrator. Jesus is now Lord of our lives.

But "legal" reality is not always "evident" reality. I'm free, but only so much as I understand my freedom and appropriate it in my life. The door to the bird cage may be open, but that means little if the bird stays put, whether because he doesn't realize he's free to go or because he refuses depart. As God's covenant people, we have been given blessings and freedoms in Christ. These include:

- *Freedom from a spirit of fear:* "For God has not given us a spirit of fear, but of power and of love and of a sound mind" (2 Tim. 1:7).

- *Freedom from worry:* "Therefore I say to you, do not worry about your life, what you will eat or what you will drink; nor about your body, what you will put on. Is not life more than food and the body more than clothing?" (Matt. 6:25).

- *Healing:* "He sent His word and healed them, and delivered them from their destructions" (Ps. 107:20).

- *Freedom from guilt and condemnation:* "For God did not send His Son into the world to condemn the world, but that the world through Him might be saved" (John 3:17).

- *Fellowship with Christ:* "God is faithful, by whom you were called into the fellowship of His Son, Jesus Christ our Lord" (1 Cor. 1:9).

- *Fellowship with other covenant people:* "But if we walk in the light as He is in the light, we have fellowship with one another, and the blood of Jesus Christ His Son cleanses us from all sin" (1 John 1:7).

Just as the caged bird had a choice, we can choose to live in this freedom or remain bound. The choice is entirely ours. The devil can't refuse to release what God says belongs to us, and God is certainly not the one keeping us from experiencing His blessings. Much of the suffering and sorrow of this life can be better understood when we have a biblical grasp both of our carnal nature and spiritual warfare. In part, what we learn through the difficulties on both of these battlefronts prepares us to rule with Christ in eternity (Rom. 5:3–5).

CHAPTER 23

Entering God's Presence

Not with the blood of goats and calves, but with
His own blood He entered the Most Holy Place once
for all, having obtained eternal redemption.

—HEBREWS 9:12

No IMAGE IN Scripture depicts in more detail the prerequisites for entering God's presence than does the Old Testament tabernacle. The manner in which it was built stands as a road map for moving from rebellion and separation from God to friendship and fellowship with Him. It all begins with God's commandment to Moses, "And let them make Me a sanctuary, that I may dwell among them. According to all that I show you, that is, the pattern of the tabernacle and the pattern of all its furnishings, just so you shall make it" (Exod. 25:8–9).

God told Moses that He would dwell among the children of Israel (His presence would be among them) and that He wanted Moses to build Him a special place of residence. The dwelling wasn't elaborate, but the way it was constructed typified what it takes to enter God's presence. The actual construction spoke of the manner in which a person was to approach God. It was a pattern for uniting with God.

A certain void in the human heart creates a restlessness and hopelessness that drives us to despair. Only when we find our way into God's presence do we understand why we have been created and find the peace we so desperately need.

First, Moses was commissioned to construct a small building with two compartments. It was to be a tent-like structure that could easily be packed up and moved quickly. The structure was to be about fifteen feet wide by forty-five feet long, and it was to be surrounded by a curtain fence seventy-five feet wide and one hundred fifty feet long[1] (Exod. 26:16). Every part of it spoke of coming into God's presence and of the Christ who could get us there. Everything outside of this enclosure represented the world affected by sin and Satan.

If a person wanted to come into God's presence, he had to begin by entering through a curtain door in the fence. Later we would learn that the curtain represented Christ being the "door" to eternal life. It is important to note that there was only one door in this white curtain fence. In the same way Jesus is the only way to get into God's presence.

There was a time in my life when I hoped there were many saviors, but that is just not the case. God's Word is clear that there is only one Savior. Jesus is the only door to the Father. Jesus Himself proclaimed, "I am the door. If anyone enters by Me, he will be saved, and will go in and out and find pasture" (John 10:9).

Once inside the tabernacle compound, a person was faced with what was called the brazen altar. It was made of bronze and stood about seven and a half feet wide and seven and a half feet long (Exod. 27:1–8). This is where animals were sacrificed so their lifeblood could make atonement for sin. Their blood would subsequently be taken from this altar and offered to God within the tabernacle.

The blood shed at the brazen altar would later be understood to represent the blood of Jesus that was offered on our behalf. The writer of Hebrews clearly saw this when he wrote, "But into the second part [inside the tent] the high priest went alone once a year, not without blood, which he offered for himself and for the people's sins committed in ignorance. . . . But Christ came as High Priest of the good things to come, with the greater and more perfect tabernacle not made with hands, that is, not of this creation. Not with the blood of goats and calves, but with His own blood He entered the Most Holy Place once for all, having obtained eternal redemption" (Heb. 9:7, 11–12).

After offering blood on the altar, a person was to proceed toward the tabernacle itself, except that there was yet another item to deal with, a washbasin called the laver. The laver was filled with water. God required physical washing before entering the tabernacle. He wanted the priests to be clean. Again, like the door and the altar, the laver also speaks of Christ. The Scripture speaks of the "washing of water by the word" (Eph. 5:26). Christ is the living Word (John 1:1, 14). Instead of washing the outer man, today we understand that God's Word washes the inner man: "But you were washed, but you were sanctified, but you were justified in the name of the Lord Jesus and by the Spirit of our God" (1 Cor. 6:11).

ENTERING THE HOLY OF HOLIES

At this point a person could enter the tabernacle. The tent-like building itself contained two rooms. The first was called the holy place and was fifteen feet wide by thirty feet long. A veil separated it from the other room called the holy of holies. Inside the holy place were three pieces of furniture that also spoke of Christ and the need for Him to lead us into God's presence. Upon entering this first of the two rooms, if you looked to the left you would see a lampstand located along the wall. It gave light to the sanctuary and represented Jesus as the light of the world. ("Then Jesus spoke to them again, saying, 'I am the light of the world. He who follows Me shall not walk in darkness, but have the light of life'" [John 8:12].)

To the right was a table called the table of showbread. It contained twelve loaves of bread, one for each of the tribes of Israel. The table spoke of Christ again, this time as the bread of life. ("And Jesus said to them, 'I am the bread of life. He who comes to Me shall never hunger, and he who believes in Me shall never thirst'" [John 6:35].)

To the back of the room and in front of the veil stood a

small altar called the altar of incense. On it burned a "sweet smelling savor" unto the Lord. In Scripture prayer is likened unto incense. The picture is one of Christ making intercession for His people while seated at the right hand of the Father. ("Therefore He is also able to save to the uttermost those who come to God through Him, since He always lives to make intercession for them" [Heb. 7:25].)

The only thing that separated the two rooms was the large heavy curtain called the veil. Behind it, in the holy of holies, was God's manifested presence. Because this place was so holy, not just anyone could go behind the veil. In fact, only priests from the tribe of Levi and of the house of Aaron had the right to get as far as we are right now. But even they couldn't go behind the veil into the presence of God. Only the high priest could do that, and he could go in only once a year: "But into the second part the high priest went alone once a year, not without blood, which he offered for himself and for the people's sins committed in ignorance" (Heb. 9:7). Again we see the importance of blood for entering God's presence.

You might be wondering what this has to do with us today. Peter tells us that in Christ we are part of the new covenant priesthood: "But you are a chosen generation, a royal priesthood, a holy nation, His own special people, that you may proclaim the praises of Him who called you out of darkness into His marvelous light" (1 Pet. 2:9). As priests of the new covenant, all believers could enter the holy place to serve the Lord. Unfortunately we could not go into the holy of holies. Only the high priest could do that. This is where Jesus comes in again. He is our high priest today. Two thousand years ago He went behind the veil on our behalf. When He did, He actually went through it, tearing it in two, thus giving the new covenant priests (you and me) direct access to the holy of holies.

This means that we have instant access to the Father twenty-four hours a day. We don't have to wait for a once-a-year invitation, and we don't need someone to go in for us. All believers have a right to talk to God any time, day or night. We read in Hebrews, "Therefore, brethren, having boldness to enter the Holiest by the blood of Jesus, by a new and living way which He consecrated for us, through the veil, that is, His flesh, and having a High Priest over the house of God" (Heb. 10:19–21; see also Heb. 6:19).

Behind the veil, in the holy of holies, sat the ark of the covenant. It was similar to a small storage chest. In it was stored the stone tablets on which the Ten Commandments were written, Aaron's rod that budded, and a jar filled with manna. On top of the ark lay the mercy seat, which was covered with gold. Over it were two gold cherubim facing each other with their wings extended to meet in the center. It was upon the mercy seat that blood from the brazen altar was sprinkled. This sprinkling of blood would reaffirm covenant relationship and call upon God's mercy.

Historically we understand that the king had to extend his mercy in order for someone to enter his presence. Bible scholar H. A. Maxwell Whyte further explains: "In Hebrews 12:24 the writer refers to the blood of Jesus by contrasting it with Abel's blood and calling it 'the blood of sprinkling, that SPEAKETH better things than that of Abel.' Whereas Abel's blood cried vengeance, Jesus' Blood cries mercy. This is what was symbolized in the Old Testament days when the mercy seat within the Holy of Holies was sprinkled with the blood of bulls and goats when the High Priest went within the Veil once a year (Hebrews 9:27)."[2]

God has extended His mercy to us through the blood of Jesus. Why? Because He loves us.

Here again at the mercy seat we find the use of substitutionary blood—the blood of animals: "And Moses took half the blood and put it in basins, and half the blood he sprinkled on the altar. Then he took the Book of the Covenant and read in the hearing of the people. And they said, 'All that the LORD has said we will do, and be obedient.' And Moses took the blood, sprinkled it on the people, and said, 'This is the blood of the covenant which the LORD has made with you according to all these words'" (Exod. 24:6–8).

In previous chapters we've discussed the use of blood in "making" a covenant. At the mercy seat we see clearly the same procedure. Moses speaks to the people that this is a covenant in blood. And the blood is sprinkled on both the altar and the people, indicating that this is a two-way agreement.

CHAPTER 24

Power in the Blood

*And they overcame him by the blood of the
Lamb and by the word of their testimony, and
they did not love their lives to the death.*

—REVELATION 12:11

W HILE IN EXILE on the Isle of Patmos John received not
only revelation concerning future events but also understanding of the blood of Jesus as a weapon against the enemy
of man's soul. Today that revelation still remains a challenge
to our thinking concerning overcoming Satan and his demons.
Certainly this chief architect of evil is no less a threat now
than he was in the days of John. Whatever was needed to fight
satanic powers in those days is still needed today. In fact, with
demonic influence growing more overt as humanity approaches
Christ's coming, every weapon available—from praise to
declaring and obeying God's Word to spending time in fasting
and prayer—is needed in order to fight the enemy successfully.

John saw that Jesus's blood provided believers with authority
against Satan (Rev. 12:11). How to appropriate that authority,
however, is not always well understood. For some, simply
saying, "I plead the blood of Jesus" (see chapter 3) when under
satanic attack is enough to send the enemy on his way. This
is not because the words "I plead the blood" are magical but
because there is true power in the blood of Jesus and often just
reminding Satan of that power is enough to make him and
his demons cower. But the power is not in the words; it is in
Christ's authority over all the power of the enemy that was
established when He shed His blood on the cross. His shed

blood established the potential for covenant relationship with God and satisfied the demands of every broken covenant. Or to put it another way, His blood dealt with sin once and for all. All power, both in heaven and earth (Matt. 28:18), belongs to Jesus, and He delegates it only to those who have made covenant with Him by simply receiving Jesus (John 1:12). With that power we have "the authority to trample on serpents and scorpions, and over all the power of the enemy, and nothing shall by any means hurt [us]" (Luke 10:19).

THE RIGHT TO RESIST SATAN

In chapter 11 we discussed the idea of "ransom" as a necessary part of the salvation process. Think of it: Christians have been "bought" out of one kingdom and placed into another. That gives them a legal right to rise up against the oppressive demands of their old taskmaster, including renouncing his accusations.

We often have a tendency to ask God to protect us and to drive the enemy away. While that has a great deal of legitimacy, God's Word also teaches that Christians have the right to use Christ's authority to resist the enemy themselves. We can literally command demons to quit harassing us and others. This measure of authority, however, cannot be used arbitrarily and independently of the Holy Spirit. Only when we are in a relationship with Jesus and following His instructions can we expect demons to give way to a "deputized" believer. Jesus said, "Without Me you can do nothing" (John 15:5). The message is clear. We must be in league with Christ to engage in any kind of spiritual warfare.

It's understandable that some Christians would think they can take authority over every demonic spirit they encounter. That's a noble idea but one that can be dangerous in light of the need for discernment. Unless a demonized person is willing to cooperate with God, no deliverance will take place. You can attempt to cast out demons all day long, but if a person does not want to change kingdoms, the demons will remain in control of that person's life. It is vital that we work directly with God to extend His kingdom and preach Jesus; otherwise all our efforts will be futile.

It is literally the indwelling Christ who gives us any ability to stand against demonic spirits, as John proclaimed: "You are of God, little children, and have overcome them, because He who is in you is greater than he who is in the world" (1 John 4:4). Not an ounce of authority would be available to us without Jesus's blood. That is why we say, "There is power in the blood of Jesus."

Only through blood does a person enter into covenant with God. Jesus shed His blood and freed us from sin, and we, in turn, must allow our hearts to be broken in surrender to Him. In this way we enter into blood covenant with Jesus and in so doing are taken out of the kingdom of darkness and translated into the kingdom of light (Col. 1:13).

Nineteenth-century evangelist R. A. Torrey wrote, "We must know the power of the blood if we are to know the power of God. Our knowing the power of the Word, the power of the Holy Spirit, and the power of prayer, is dependent upon our knowing the power of the blood of Christ."[1]

No other weapon in the Christian's arsenal is more important or more powerful than Jesus's blood. We can only overcome the enemy through the blood of the Lamb. John wrote, "And they [God's people] overcame him [Satan and his demons] by the blood of the Lamb" (Rev. 12:11). It is important for Christians to reject mystical notions about Jesus's blood and discover how and why it is such a valuable weapon in spiritual warfare.

Christ's blood destroys two major areas of bondage: it brings release from satanic bondage and control, and it brings release from the power of sin. It also unites us in Christ and reconciles us to God, as the apostle Paul explains: "But now in Christ Jesus you who once were far off have been brought near by the blood of Christ. For He Himself is our peace, who has made both one, and has broken down the middle wall of separation, having abolished in His flesh the enmity, that is, the law of commandments contained in ordinances, so as to create in Himself one new man from the two, thus making peace, and that He might reconcile them both to God in one body through the cross, thereby putting to death the enmity. And He came and preached peace to you who were afar off and to those who were near" (Eph. 2:13–17).

A RESTORED EARTH

By way of review, recall that Adam's sin destroyed our relationship with God and brought humanity under the control of Satan and his demons. In the process Satan literally became the ruler of this world. Satan confronted Jesus claiming this right to rulership. ("And the devil said to Him, 'All this authority I will give You, and their glory; for this has been delivered to me, and I give it to whomever I wish'" [Luke 4:6].) God didn't give this planet to the enemy. Adam in his disobedience did. Because of that humanity fell under Satan's influence: "We know that we are of God, and the whole world lies under the sway of the wicked one" (1 John 5:19).

God wants Planet Earth back. In truth it always has been His; the psalmist proclaimed, "The earth is the LORD's, and all its fullness, the world and those who dwell therein" (Ps. 24:1). But the heart of mankind has been far from God. To get us back to Himself and the planet back into our hands, God was willing to pay an unimaginable price.

God's plan was to re-covenant with humanity. His intention has always been to bring us back by agreement. Blood was to form the basis of this agreement. It was to be the bonding agent in a lasting relationship with Himself. By making a blood covenant with man, God would provide a way for our permanent release from the power and control of the enemy. That's why when the enemy tries to regain control of a person's life, that individual can simply tell him, "I don't belong to you anymore.

I'm in covenant with God through Christ's blood. You can't touch me. I am not under your authority."

By grasping the significance and reality of this new relationship with God, which brings freedom from the enemy's control, one can go on to further demand release from all effects of the enemy's kingdom, including worry, fear, anxiety, and a host of other emotional problems that are not a part of the new kingdom. (Some emotional difficulties seem to linger and refuse to give way to the power of God. But when we remain persistent, believing that we have victory through Jesus's blood, they will yield in time. Don't give up.)

Release from the enemy and continued protection from his influence are powerfully portrayed by the Passover. Remember that when the children of Israel were moving from Egypt to Canaan, Pharaoh hindered them and God decided to severely judge the land. To avoid judgment themselves, the Israelites needed to reconfirm covenant relationship with God. Since the original covenant was made in blood, they needed to reestablish it in blood. Those willing to do so placed blood on the doorposts of their homes. When the death angel passed by, only those who had covenanted with God were spared judgment.

In like manner today entering into blood covenant with God both saves us from His judgment and from satanic control. Freedom is granted on the basis of a new alliance, one in which Christ guarantees safety and protection just as God did in the initial covenant He made with the children of Israel.

In the new covenant, however, each individual must covenant with God on his own. Nobody can do it for another person, and failure to enter into covenant relationship with God keeps a person under the influence of the enemy. Again the Scripture says, "We know that we are of God, and the whole world lies under the sway of the wicked one" (1 John 5:19).

Sin ruins, and God in His holiness has no alternative but to judge sin. It would be unthinkable for Him to allow sin to continue its destruction on mankind. God will not abide in sin's presence, and when it affects His own people, He is obligated to do something about it. Satan knows this and acts as the neighborhood brat who constantly knocks at other parents' doors tattling on their kids. He is an "accuser of the brethren," but his accusations are not always false. When he accuses a person before God, he knows he can't lie to the court of heaven, so he accuses people of things of which they are guilty. At that point God must deal with the complaint, even if it comes from Satan. But if He dealt with us according to our sins, we would be in continuous trouble. That is why the Scripture affirms that "He has not dealt with us according to our sins, nor punished us according to our iniquities. For as the heavens are high above the earth, so great is His mercy toward those who fear Him" (Ps. 103:10–11).

God forgives us when we confess our wrongs and repent, but our human concept of forgiveness is often much different from His. When we think of forgiveness, we generally think of simply forgetting a trespass. Not so with God. The covenant was made in blood, and if failed, it must be paid for in blood. Therefore, God's forgiveness is contingent on keeping our hearts in covenant relationship with Him. Our obligation is to own up to the offense and to receive His help in living correctly. When we come back to this point, the enemy's accusations become worthless, because "if we confess our sins, He is faithful and just to forgive us our sins and to cleanse us from all unrighteousness" (1 John 1:9). By repenting (which is to change one's mind and direction), a person stays free from sin and, as a result, can reject both the enemy's real and false accusations.

There is a destructive mentality sometimes found in the body of Christ that arbitrarily dismisses sin with the attitude that if a person is sorry, he should be forgiven. While in most cases this is close to the proper approach, forgiveness does not always mean that the person with the sin can continue on as if nothing happened. Embracing someone with forgiveness is one thing, but restoring him to his previous position in Christ's body is another. The idea is not one of punishment or retribution. It is a principle that safeguards the offender and those around him. True restoration says, "You need to take some time off in order to rebuild an area of your life in which you have become vulnerable to sin."

OVERCOMING GUILT AND CONDEMNATION

Nobody likes guilt, but true guilt can actually be a friend. It is a warning sign that danger is near. Certainly one is bound to feel miserable when guilt is present. Regardless, true guilt must be dealt with in a sensitive manner. Failure to do so hardens the spirit in such a way that it becomes numb to future warnings. The Scripture refers to this as a "conscience seared with a hot iron" (1 Tim. 4:2). Continually rejecting the warning light eventually makes it of no effect.

False guilt and false condemnation, on the other hand, can be very real enemies. They are the counterfeits to true conviction, and we need the power of the blood to fight them effectively. They shape human emotions in a destructive way and were never intended to be a part of a person's life. Jesus said, "For God did not send His Son into the world to condemn the world, but that the world through Him might be saved" (John 3:17). Unless guilt and condemnation are dealt with properly, a person remains vulnerable to deep emotional difficulties. The enemy's accusations are meant to bring deep feelings of guilt, condemnation, and hopelessness. We can resist this attack if we know that we stand justified before God. Saying "I plead the blood of Jesus" will do little as a warfare tactic if one is ignorant of the reasons Christ's blood makes us free. If you remember nothing else, remember this: someone else paid the price for your sin. That act alone purchased your freedom. You can reject the enemy's condemnation simply because Jesus died and you have entered into covenant with Him. This is what takes away the condemnation, but you have to know it.

I want to make one last point about pleading the blood

of Jesus. The new covenant gives us the right to use Jesus's authority. Because we stand in Christ's authority, we should have no fear when confronting demonic spirits. Jesus triumphed over them on the cross and made a spectacle of them (Col. 2:15). We can and should remind Satan of the power of Jesus's blood. There is nothing wrong with saying "I plead the blood of Jesus" when under spiritual attack. The key, again, is understanding that there is nothing magical in the statement; the power is in the authority conferred to us through the shedding of Christ's blood. When we plead the blood, we are acknowledging that we are not worthy to be a part of God's kingdom, but His blood has made us worthy. And as priests of this new blood covenant in Christ, we have been given authority to deal with the enemy.

Scripture teaches that Jesus took our condemnation. He paid the price of sin. The result is freedom from both sin and Satan. Recognizing that Christians are not free to use God's grace as a license to sin, we understand we are free from the need to pay for our own sin personally. We also know that we are free from sin's eternal consequences, from both the presence and power of sin.

When the enemy comes to accuse, you can stand confident in the fact that your sins have been washed away if you have confessed your sin before God and acknowledged that the blood of Jesus has dealt with your sin. When that is done, you can take joy in God's promise of forgiveness. The enemy will still try to needle you, but all you need to do is keep your attention on the blood of Jesus.

Again, H. A. Maxwell Whyte writes: "A pastor of our acquaintance, who was at one time a naturopath doctor, once contracted ptomaine poisoning. He placed his hands upon his own body and for twenty minutes pleaded the Blood of Jesus, saying, 'I plead the Blood of Jesus,' over and over again. The result of this attack on Satan's effort to destroy him was that he was completely healed. Others find that the simple repetition of the one word 'Blood' is sufficient. There are no rules; it is the simple offering of the Blood of Jesus in faith, as priests of the New Testament, which brings results. God will hear the Blood-cry and will respect that which it has purchased for us."[2] There are no rules or specific words to proclaim because pleading Jesus's blood is simply acknowledging that we know what His blood has accomplished, both in establishing the new covenant and cleansing us of sin.

CHAPTER 25

Counterfeit Covenants

*And no wonder! For Satan himself transforms
himself into an angel of light.*

—2 CORINTHIANS 11:14

S ATAN AND HIS demons are real. Because we usually cannot
physically see or hear them, it is easy to assume they may
be nothing more than figments of human imagination. But
Jesus dealt with demons as real beings. Many Christians, especially those in leadership, encounter demon spirits and see them
manifest in people in what is typically called "demon possession." You don't have to see too many cases of demon possession
before you realize that the stories of exorcism in the Bible are
true accounts.

But who is Satan? It is quite possible that humans and angels
had much to do with each other originally. This, of course, is
speculation, but we do know from the chronicle of Adam and
Eve that Satan was on earth during the early days of human
existence. And he and his demons are still here today. (The
devil would love for Christians to think he doesn't exist, but
Ephesians 6:12 says we wrestle not against flesh and blood but
against a host of wicked demonic spirits.) So the question is
not, "Does Satan exist?" But, "Why is he here, and what is he
trying to accomplish?"

It appears that the enemy has but one goal, and that is to
destroy the human race. As a result, there is a very real though
unseen war raging. Because it is unseen, we often say it is
fought by faith in Jesus and the Scriptures.

Fighting the good fight of faith, as Paul did, demands

knowledge of the enemy and an understanding of his warfare tactics. The battle takes place on two fronts. First, we war against the flesh. This is not necessarily demonic, but demons use the flesh when they see an opportunity. Paul wrote, "For what I am doing, I do not understand. For what I will to do, that I do not practice; but what I hate, that I do" (Rom. 7:15). In other words, he was saying, "I don't always do what I know is right to do, and the things that I know are wrong are what I often do." Sound familiar?

But then there is a second battlefront where we war directly against the enemy. It is easy to say, "I really don't want to get involved with that demon stuff," as if the whole war would simply go away if we didn't think about it. But ignorance gives Satan and his demons the advantage. Jesus said, "When anyone hears the word of the kingdom, and *does not understand it*, then the wicked one comes and snatches away what was sown in his heart" (Matt. 13:19, emphasis added). God's people are literally destroyed for lack of knowledge (Hosea 4:6).

Paul exhorts Christians to "put on the whole armor of God, that [we] may be able to stand against the wiles of the devil" (Eph. 6:11). James instructs us, "Submit to God. Resist the devil and he will flee from you" (James 4:7). Peter admonishes: "Be sober, be vigilant; because your adversary the devil walks about like a roaring lion, seeking whom he may devour" (1 Pet. 5:8). "Ignore the enemy and the invisible war he's waging" isn't one of the options.

SATAN'S TACTICS

The devil uses two powerful tactics of warfare against Christians. (He has more than two devices, of course, but these are so effective he uses them often.) First is discouragement. Simply living in a cursed world, in bodies of clay, and subject to the influences of the enemy will eventually wear a person down mentally, emotionally, and spiritually. Paul warned Timothy about this, saying, "Now the Spirit expressly says that in latter times some will depart from the faith, giving heed to deceiving spirits and doctrines of demons" (1 Tim. 4:1).

The second tactic is deception. Satan can do very little to humanity other than to work through the human mind. Through deception he has become the ruler of this present world. By manipulating and controlling the way we think, he controls this planet. We choose to sin, and we are responsible for our actions, but Satan is often the one who plants the idea in our minds.

This is what he did in the Garden of Eden. After God told Adam and Eve not to eat of the tree of the knowledge of good and evil, Satan came along and asked Eve, "Has God indeed said, 'You shall not eat of every tree of the garden'?" (Gen. 3:1). By questioning God, Satan caused Eve to doubt God's word and as a result to disobey His command.

Many of the enemy's lies come in half-truths. For instance, you've probably heard people say, "I don't go for all that shouting and praising the Lord stuff. God expects us to be reverent." It's true that God expects us to be reverent, but that doesn't negate the power of praise. The Bible says, "Be glad in the LORD and rejoice, you righteous; and shout for joy, all you upright in heart!" (Ps. 32:11). It's not either-or as Satan would like us to think. We can honor God's holiness and sing His praises. Besides hating Jesus's blood, Satan hates praise and would love to keep it from your lips.

Here's another common one: "I don't believe we should talk about demons. We need to take responsibility for the way we live our own lives." Do we need to take responsibility for the way we live? Absolutely! But the Scriptures also tell us not to be ignorant of Satan's devices (2 Cor. 2:11). Again, the truth is being distorted.

Deception mixes truth with the counterfeit. In some cases the thoughts and ideas that cause deception are so close to real truth that it is almost impossible to tell the difference. For instance, there are those who put the article *a* in front of the word *God* in John 1:1 thereby changing the meaning in such a way that they claim Jesus is not God manifest in the flesh. The Bible says, "In the beginning was the Word, and the Word was with God, and the Word was God" (John 1:1). The Word was God, not "a god." In the Greek the word *God* in the phrase "was God" is a predicate nominative and does not need an article such as *a* in front of it for clarification. John wrote plainly that Jesus was God.

In the Book of Isaiah when Satan said, "I will be like the Most High," he sought to counterfeit God. Perhaps as he looked over God's magnificent universe, he said, "Wow, that's impressive. I'd like to have that as my own." But notice in Isaiah's account that the enemy did not say, "I will be God." He said, "I will be *like* God" (Isa. 14:14, emphasis added). He's an imitator, an impostor. All he can do is counterfeit the real thing.

Satan even attempts to pervert what God has established through blood covenant. There are cultures around the world that think they can only escape satanic oppression by offering human and animal sacrifices to appease Satan. We also see a demonic perversion of blood covenant among gangs. Gang members relate to each other on the basis of family. Loyalty is vitally important, and death is the consequence of disloyalty. Once in a gang, often it's for life. "Blood in, blood out," the saying goes. This makes it virtually impossible for some people to leave gangs.

The covenant God makes with us does not leave us in bondage and fear. It liberates and empowers. Of course, that is the last thing the enemy wants us to know—that we have power to defeat him through the blood of Jesus.

CHAPTER 26

Breaking the New Covenant

And the uncircumcised male child, who is not circumcised
in the flesh of his foreskin, that person shall be cut
off from his people; he has broken My covenant.

—Genesis 17:14

WHEN A PERSON signs a blood covenant with God and
then breaks it, he has nothing to offer but his life as
a payment for his sin. He's in serious trouble. (See Jeremiah
34:18–20.) The question is, can a person get out of this trouble?
Or in other words, can he be forgiven? The answer is yes, but
the process begins with the same broken and contrite heart that
was necessary to begin the relationship. The Bible says, "The
LORD is near to those who have a broken heart, and saves such
as have a contrite spirit" (Ps. 34:18). And, "The sacrifices of
God are a broken spirit, a broken and a contrite heart—these,
O God, You will not despise" (Ps. 51:17).

It is this attitude before God that represents "circumcision."
I want to mention again that all too often we are tempted to try
to make up for the sin through self-effort. It seems reasonable
to make things right by doing something to correct the wrong.
Certainly we are to right our wrongs when possible, but not by
performing a bunch of righteous acts to show God we are truly
sorry. That doesn't work with God. We can get ourselves into
messes, but we can't straighten them out on our own. Certainly
right actions are important, but not as a measure for securing
God's favor or making up for past failure. His favor is secured
through Jesus's work on the cross and is extended to us through
Christ as we humble ourselves before Him.

Like a child who has done wrong and comes crying to his parents, God wants His people to run into His arms and say, "Daddy, I've really messed up." He wants us to admit our wrong, to be honest about it. This is brokenness! When we acknowledge our sin to Him, God will listen. The Bible says, "If we confess our sins, He is faithful and just to forgive us our sins and to cleanse us from all unrighteousness" (1 John 1:9).

Confession gets the problem out in the open where it can be dealt with. God wants to talk with us about everything in life, including our failures. He says, "Come now, and let us reason together...though your sins are like scarlet, they shall be as white as snow; though they are red like crimson, they shall be as wool" (Isa. 1:18).

Psalm 66:18 is a sobering verse: "If I regard iniquity in my heart, the Lord will not hear." Those who claim they have no sin or who insist on justifying their sin cannot get God's attention. The Bible says, "If we say that we have not sinned, we make Him a liar, and His word is not in us" (1 John 1:10). If we want God's help, we must bring our issues to Him.

Embarrassment, guilt, and shame prevent many from pouring their hearts out to God. These things keep people from the brokenness that serves to make things right. Some hate the idea of confessing their sins because they see it as groveling before an austere and demanding God. Nothing could be further from the truth. The image of a cold and heartless authority figure has to be destroyed if we are going to find the forgiveness we so desperately need. It must then be replaced with an understanding of a true, loving father, because that is who God is.

"PRACTICING" SIN

John writes, "Whoever has been born of God does not sin, for His seed remains in him; and he cannot sin, because he has been born of God" (1 John 3:9). It almost sounds as if God is saying that once you are saved, you will never sin again. John has already indicated that the opposite is true: "If we say that we have no sin, we deceive ourselves, and the truth is not in us" (1 John 1:8).

As James says, "We all stumble in many things" (James 3:2). John's message in 1 John 3:9 addresses the power of sin that compels people to do wrong things. It has to do with "practicing" sin. John goes on to acknowledge that the power to keep sin away comes as a result of the indwelling Christ, saying, "He who is in you is greater than he who is in the world" (1 John 4:4). Tripping and falling into sin is quite different than practicing it.

Occasionally we all slip and fall. We all make mistakes. I say this not to justify continuing in sin but to acknowledge the reality we all face. If, or when, I find that I have failed, I need to follow the biblical process to get back on track with God, which begins with confession. By going to God humbly, you will find Him willing and ready to forgive. That is His nature. It is who He is—the God who forgives.

UNPARDONABLE SIN

Is there a sin that God will not forgive? God's Word tells us that He will not forgive the sin of blasphemy against the Holy Spirit: "Therefore I say to you, every sin and blasphemy will be forgiven men, but the blasphemy against the Spirit will not be forgiven men" (Matt. 12:31). To bitterly denounce the Holy Spirit, especially by attributing His workings to the devil, is unpardonable. This sin seems to involve some kind of hardness toward God.

The Book of Hebrews describes a person who has sinned in this way: "For it is impossible for those who were once enlightened, and have tasted the heavenly gift, and have become partakers of the Holy Spirit, and have tasted the good word of God and the powers of the age to come, if they fall away, to renew them again to repentance, since they crucify again for themselves the Son of God, and put Him to an open shame"

(Heb. 6:4–6). It goes on to say, "Of how much worse punishment, do you suppose, will he be thought worthy who has trampled the Son of God underfoot, counted the blood of the covenant by which he was sanctified a common thing, and insulted the Spirit of grace?" (Heb. 10:29).

These are not simply wayward people who for a time have again become self-centered and rebellious, like the prodigal son. Rather, these are people who no longer are interested in God's grace and want nothing to do with Him. The pharaoh of Moses's day had a heart so hard that he would not listen to God. And as God continued to press Pharaoh, his heart grew even harder (Exod. 8:15, 32).

Many Christians worry that they may have committed the unpardonable sin. There is a simple test, and it comes in the form of a question. If you fear all hope for you is lost because of the way you have lived or because of what you once said to or about God, ask yourself this: "Do I want God now?" If you can sincerely say yes, you have not committed the unpardonable sin. If you have a genuine desire to be right with God, you still can be.

The reason we know this is because the very desire to know God comes from Him. If God doesn't draw a person's heart toward Himself, that person will not consider his need for God. He will not want a relationship with God, and he certainly will not seek Him. (See Romans 3:11.) Jesus said, "No one can come to Me unless the Father who sent Me draws him; and I will raise him up at the last day" (John 6:44).

If you care enough about God to even ask, "Have I grieved the Holy Spirit beyond repair?," you haven't. Just as in a struggling marriage, as long as both parties want reconciliation, there is hope.

Breaking covenant with God is not the same as falling into the sin that so easily besets us (Heb. 12:1). When rebellion is allowed to remain, we are breaking covenant, not merely falling into sin. Breaking covenant casts God off and wishes for a divorce from Him. Although most Christians would never consider doing such a thing, some who backslide may come very close. Only God knows for sure the real condition of a person's heart.

When we sin, we are failing to keep the stipulations of the agreement with God. A sinful act does not destroy the covenant a person has with God. That happens only through open rebellion from a heart that wants no part of the agreement and remains that way.

CHAPTER 27

The Covenant of Promise

Then He brought him outside and said, "Look now toward heaven, and count the stars if you are able to number them." And He said to him, "So shall your descendants be."

—GENESIS 15:5

THE COVENANT GOD made with Abraham in Genesis 15 and 17 is often called the covenant of promise. Some assume that the whole Abrahamic covenant was one of promise and that such a covenant, by its nature, would not reflect the mutuality normally found in other kinds of covenants. It has been thought that the Abrahamic covenant was a unilateral agreement without any consent from Abraham. But that is only true of the "promise" part.

God told Abraham, "Your descendants shall be as the dust of the earth; you shall spread abroad to the west and the east, to the north and the south; and in you and in your seed all the families of the earth shall be blessed" (Gen. 28:14). This promise was not part of the covenant God made with him. There was nothing Abraham could or could not do to see the promise fulfilled. That is, it was void of stipulations. In that manner it was outside of covenant, which always carries stipulations.

Yet the promise to Abraham was critical in fulfilling God's redemptive plan. This is not to diminish the need for righteousness that the Law brought to the fore, but the promise to Abraham outweighs the Law by light-years. In fact, if a person really wants to know what God is up to, he or she needs to start with the promise to Abraham and then go to the Law.

The promise part of God's agreement with Abraham was

179

formulated in God's mind before the foundation of the world. God didn't just suddenly think of it when He initiated the Abrahamic covenant. God decided that the fulfilment of the promise would be Jesus. Scripture says, "He [Christ] indeed was foreordained before the foundation of the world, but was manifest in these last times for you" (1 Pet. 1:20).

God's plan for restoring humanity to Himself was to present another man who could undo the damage the first man, Adam, had done. This new man needed to be born through a special genealogy under God's direct influence, and God chose Abraham to begin that lineage. The promise was made to mankind before Abraham even arrived on the scene (it was actually made to Jesus on behalf of mankind), as the following passage so succinctly explains:

> Brothers and sisters, let us think in human terms: Even an agreement made between two persons is firm. After that agreement is accepted by both people, no one can stop it or add anything to it. God made promises both to Abraham and to his descendant. God did not say, "and to your descendants." That would mean many people. But God said, "and to your descendant." That means only one person; that person is Christ. This is what I mean: God had an agreement with Abraham and promised to keep it. The law, which came four hundred thirty years later, cannot change that agreement and so destroy God's promise to Abraham. If the law could give us Abraham's blessing, then the promise would not be necessary. But that is not possible, because God freely gave his blessings to Abraham through the promise he had made.
>
> —GALATIANS 3:15–18, NCV

Notice carefully that God makes two promises in the above verses, one to Abraham and the other to "his descendant," Jesus. In covenanting with Abraham, God not only reveals the promise of Jesus but also promises Abraham that the fulfillment of the promise would come "through" his seed.

Christ is the fulfillment of God's promise to all humanity "declared" through Abraham but determined long before Abraham was born. For God to be able to deliver the promise He would have to find someone, an earthly human being, who would respond to Him so the promise would be confirmed. The nature of rebellion, however, caused antagonism toward God. Someone had to be willing to come out of rebellion and covenant with God for the promise to manifest.

Before God was willing to announce the promise through Abraham and sign an agreement with him, He had to be sure that Abraham would participate willingly. Abraham had to believe God, which eventually happened: "And he [Abraham] believed in the LORD, and He accounted it to him for righteousness" (Gen. 15:6).

From the beginning the promise of humanity's restoration was secure; that is, God would have fulfilled it whether or not Abraham responded to Him. If Abraham had been unbelieving, God would have moved on until He found a willing person. "For the eyes of the LORD run to and fro throughout the whole earth, to show Himself strong on behalf of those whose heart is loyal to Him" (2 Chron. 16:9). God is still searching today, looking for willing people to enter into covenant relationship with Him.

Once God found Abraham and made His promise known to him, Abraham was then required to enter into covenant relationship. The promise was not the covenant but rather a part of it. If a person wants to be involved in what God is going to do in the earth, he has to covenant with Him. So while the promise was unilateral, the covenant God made with Abraham was not. Abraham had to agree. If he failed to respond positively to God, the covenant would have ceased to exist through him, but not the promise. God would have fulfilled it through someone else.

As discussed earlier, some Bible scholars conclude that the Abrahamic covenant was *unilateral*, that it wasn't a true *agreement,* because Abraham had nothing to say about it. This conclusion is based on God passing between the halves of the animals as His signature on the agreement while Abraham slept. This is thought to mean that the agreement was aside from Abraham's consent. The thinking appears to be that God really made two covenants with Abraham, one in Genesis 15 and the other in Genesis 17. This, however, could not be the case. God had only one covenant with Abraham. Nowhere in Scripture do we find more than one Abrahamic covenant. God signed the agreement in Genesis 15, and Abraham signed it in Genesis 17.

AN INNER TRANSFORMATION

The Old Testament Law, which is basically the Ten Commandments, is often thought of as the essence of covenant relationship with God. In reality it was only a feature instituted under Moses because of the hardness of the people's hearts. The Law established what was necessary to maintain relationships, and in the process it sustains cultures. The righteousness of the Law was to remain forever, because it is the basis of all relationships. Without it the human race would quickly destroy itself.

But because of the Law's dictatorial nature it was not easily kept. (It only feels dictatorial because of rebellion. Outside of rebellion we would see it as something necessary for the world to run properly.) God knew that true righteousness could not be motivated by fear. It would need to come from an inner transformation. Mankind must want righteousness if it is to be manifested as a lifestyle. And as I have stated, this would happen only through the indwelling Christ. Again, we read in Hebrews: "For this is the covenant that I will make with the house of Israel after those days, says the LORD: I will put My laws in their mind and write them on their hearts; and I will be their God, and they shall be My people" (Heb. 8:10).

"Christ in us" would be our only hope of real righteousness

(Col. 1:27). Only He could put the determination to do God's will inside the human heart. A person, however, would have to agree to allow God's will to be done (Phil. 2:13; Heb. 13:21).

And so the Law showed what was necessary to live in ways that would preserve the planet, but only through Jesus would mankind find the power to keep the Law. Today it is the law of Christ (Gal. 6:2) that provides the righteousness that not only fulfills the Old Testament Law but also causes a person to "want" to do what is right.

What was the purpose of the Law? "It was added because of transgressions, till the Seed should come.... The law was our tutor to *bring* us to Christ" (Gal. 3:19, 24).

Was the Law against the promises of God? "Certainly not! For if there had been a law given which could have given life, truly righteousness would have been by the law" (v. 21).

It is often thought that a covenant is the same as a last will and testament. A will or testament is really only part of the covenant and not the covenant itself. But the covenant does grant us an inheritance. The apostle Paul wrote, "For if the inheritance is of the law, it is no longer of promise; but God gave it to Abraham by promise" (v. 18).

If the covenant with Abraham was fulfilled in Christ, what then does Scripture say about Gentiles? "And the Scripture, foreseeing that God would justify the nations by faith, preached the gospel to Abraham beforehand, saying, *"In you all the nations shall be blessed"* (v. 8, emphasis added). Paul goes on to say, "That the blessing of Abraham might come upon the Gentiles in Christ Jesus, that we might receive the promise of the Spirit through faith" (v. 14). Later still Paul writes, "Having predestined us to adoption as sons by Jesus Christ to Himself, according to the good pleasure of His will" (Eph. 1:5). Grafting in the Gentiles was always part of God's eternal redemption plan.

CHAPTER 28

The Wonder of Being "in Christ"

Blessed be the God and Father of our Lord Jesus Christ, who has blessed us with every spiritual blessing in the heavenly places in Christ.

—Ephesians 1:3

I F WE TAKE everything written in the previous chapters and sum it all up, it comes down to just one truth—we are now in Christ. This was God's ultimate plan for humanity—for us to be closer to Him than to anyone or anything else, even a spouse. He wants us so near to Him that He said, "Eye has not seen, nor ear heard, nor have entered into the heart of man the things which God has prepared for those who love Him" (1 Cor. 2:9). Don't miss God's point in all of this: He wants this relationship for us in the here and now and not just after we have entered heaven.

One day my friend Jim Ayars and I were discussing the concept of being "in Christ." I was looking for an illustration to convey the point in a way that was easy to understand. He used this example: If you were to take a small stick and begin beating it against something hard, it would eventually break. But if you were to take a hollow pipe and do the same, it would withstand the blows. Yet if you take the stick and place it inside the pipe and continue the pounding, what would happen to the stick? It would be protected inside the pipe.

Another illustration might help to further clarify the point: Can airplanes fly? The law of gravity says they can't, because objects that are heavier than air must fall, not fly. And everyone knows airplanes are heavier than air. But can airplanes fly? You bet they can! The law of aerodynamics says they not only can fly, but also they *must*, because the law states that if an object heavier than air attains sufficient speed, it will fly. The law of gravity is overruled by the law of aerodynamics.

Now suppose there are two airplanes. The first represents the flesh in which we live. Its engines are dead and cannot be used. I can sit in the plane as long as I want and it isn't going anywhere. I can get out of it and start pushing, but that will not get it into the air. However, in the second plane there is full power. Christ is in control, and the plane will fly. He has invited me into His "airplane," and I am able to fly with Him because His invitation came with no stipulations. There were no prerequisites to getting into the airplane. All we had to do was get in.

We don't have to be good first. Consider what happens when we enter Jesus's "plane":

1. We please Him by accepting His invitation to come aboard.

2. We take our seats not because of what we have done but because of what He did to ensure we were able to board the plane. He and His airplane are perfect in every way, and nothing imperfect is allowed to enter His domain, so we needed Him to make a way for us to come aboard His plane. We could not have done it on our own.

3. Once on board He sets about restoring our lives and healing our wounds.

4. Because He knows we have little ability to please Him, He offers us a relationship and constantly helps us to become more like He is.

When we accept Jesus's invitation onto His "plane," we are "in Christ." Those two words are at the heart of both the gospel and the everlasting covenant. The phrases "in Christ" and "God in Christ" are found almost three hundred times in the New Testament, which indicates how key this is to our understanding of the work of Christ in all aspects of redemption and reconciliation.

In the next chapter I explain what it means to have "Christ in us." I wrote it to encourage those who think we have to work hard to please a God who gets more than a little irritated when we fail to live up to His standards. God knows how hard it is for us to live a "good" life, and He offers His help by way of the Holy Spirit to lovingly strengthen us when we need it. But all of this must be prefaced by being "in union" with the person and work of Jesus. In other words, there is no "Christ in us" unless we are first and foremost "in Christ."

GETTING OUT OF ADAM

God deals with us not only as individuals but also corporately as the human race. In reading the Scriptures, be aware that a major theme has to do with God's work with us as people in general. We can trace the "all men" expression to the Garden of Eden, where the whole human race fell with Adam.

> Therefore, just as through one man sin entered the world, and death through sin, and thus death spread to all men, because all sinned.
>
> —Romans 5:12

> For as by one man's disobedience many were made sinners, so also by one Man's obedience many will be made righteous.
>
> —Romans 5:19

> For as in Adam all die, even so in Christ all shall be made alive.
>
> —1 Corinthians 15:22

We are fallen because we were "in Adam" in the beginning not just as individuals but as part of the human race. The sin in Adam was reproduced in all of his offspring, separating us from the life that is in Christ. Psalm 51:5 says, "Behold, I was brought forth in iniquity, and in sin my mother conceived me."

We were made sinners in Adam's one act of disobedience. This brought us under the sentence of death, as we read in Romans 5:14–15: "Nevertheless death reigned from Adam to Moses, even over those who had not sinned according to the likeness of the transgression of Adam, who is a type of Him who was to come. But the free gift is not like the offense. For if by the one man's offense many died, much more the grace of God and the gift by the grace of the one Man, Jesus Christ, abounded to many."

Adam's sin also brought us under judgment and condemnation:

> (And the gift is not like that which came through the one who sinned. For the judgment which came from one offense resulted in condemnation, but the free gift which came from many offenses resulted in justification. For if by the one man's offense death reigned through the one, much more those who receive abundance of grace and of the gift of righteousness will reign in life through the One, Jesus Christ.)
>
> Therefore, as through one man's offense judgment came to all men, resulting in condemnation, even so through one Man's righteous act the free gift came to all men, resulting in justification of life.
>
> —ROMANS 5:16–18

Now "in Adam," the whole world lies under the influence of Satan and his demons, as 1 John 5:19 tells us: "We know that we are of God, and the whole world lies under the sway of the wicked one." But John follows up quickly to say that those who entered into the new covenant with God are now "in Christ." He writes in the next verse, "And we know that the Son of God has come and has given us an understanding, that we may know Him who is true; and we are in Him who is true, in His Son Jesus Christ. This is the true God and eternal life" (v. 20).

Being "in Christ" means we are no longer "under Satan." We have passed from the kingdom of death and darkness into the kingdom of light and life. We have been freed from Satan's right to dominate us (Col. 1:12–18).

God's solution to the fall was to replace the first Adam with the second Adam, His own Son, Jesus Christ. God foresaw mankind's calamitous fall and decided to reconcile us back to Himself "in" His Son.

> And you, who once were alienated and enemies in your mind by wicked works, yet now He has reconciled in the body of His flesh through death, to present you holy, and blameless, and above reproach in His sight—if indeed you continue in the faith, grounded and steadfast, and are not moved away from the hope of the gospel which you heard.
>
> —Colossians 1:21–23

> Just as He chose us in Him before the foundation of the world, that we should be holy and without blame before Him in love [He decided then to adopt us as children to Himself by Jesus Christ], having predestined us to adoption as sons by Jesus Christ to Himself, according to the good pleasure of His will, to the praise of the glory of His grace, by which He made us accepted *in the Beloved*.
>
> —Ephesians 1:4–6, emphasis added

The mystery of His will from before the beginning of the world was to unite as one "all things *in Christ*, both which are in heaven and which are on earth—*in Him*" (Eph. 1:10, emphasis added). Once we have been reconciled to Him and are "in Christ," we become brand new. Even though we may not look any different on the outside, in the spirit we have been completely transformed, and God sees us totally differently. I want to spend the rest of this chapter examining how God sees us and how our lives change when we are "in Christ."

WE ARE BROUGHT NEAR TO GOD'S HEART "IN CHRIST"

"But now in Christ Jesus you who once were far off have been brought near by the blood of Christ" (Eph. 2:13). If you've ever had that "far off" feeling, especially after you came to Christ, look carefully at this verse. It says we have come into Christ by His blood. This statement is profound. You didn't come into Jesus by something you did. You came into His kingdom, His favor, His life, His grace, and His love by what *He* did.

Don't argue against His love for you because of the way you feel. Not one single saint of God has felt any different from you. All of God's people have trouble accepting His grace because of how far Adam strayed from Him. (See Romans 5:15.)

I like the way A. W. Tozer expressed this truth:

> The living God did not degrade Himself by this condescension. He did not in any sense make Himself to be less than God.
>
> He remained ever God and everything else remained not God. The gulf still existed even after Jesus Christ had become man and had dwelt among us. Instead of God degrading Himself when He became man, by the act of Incarnation He elevated mankind to Himself.
>
> It is plain in the Athanasian Creed that the early church fathers were very cautious at this point of doctrine. They would not allow us to believe that God, in the Incarnation, became flesh by coming down of the Deity into flesh; but rather by the taking up of mankind into God.
>
> Thus we do not degrade God but we elevate man—and that is the wonder of redemption.[1]

"IN HIM" WE HAVE *FORGIVENESS* OF SINS

"In Him we have redemption through His blood, the forgiveness of sins" (Eph. 1:7). In order for us to receive Jesus and be brought "into" Him, He would have to do something about our sin. Since we were "bound" in sin and could not do anything on our own, He would have to make us different so that sin would not stand in the way of our relationship with Him. And He did this through the substitutionary work of Jesus.[2]

On January 15, 2009, Captain Chesley Burnett "Sully" Sullenberger, pilot of US Airways Flight 1549, landed his plane in the Hudson River near New York City after it struck a flock of birds soon after takeoff. Sullenberger's training and remarkable calmness allowed him to land the plane in the water without losing any of the 155 passengers and crew.[3] I'm sure that not a single person had the slightest desire to rob Sullenberger of the joy he felt at not losing a single person under his care.

So it is with God. Don't rob Him of His joy in what Christ accomplished for you on the cross. That joy is to see you understand that you are completely forgiven and realize that He has nothing against you when you enter His presence.

WE ARE MADE THE *RIGHTEOUSNESS OF GOD* "IN HIM"

"For He made Him who knew no sin to be sin for us, that we might become the righteousness of God in Him" (2 Cor. 5:21). Christ took on the penalty we deserved. He was condemned for our sins that we might be justified by His righteousness. He had no part in our sinfulness, and we had no part in His righteousness, yet He bridged the divide when He hung on the cross. He suffered for us that we might partake in His righteousness.

Here is an illustration to help make the point. Suppose a company hires a contractor to do a job that requires him to have many workers. When the contractor arrives with his team of workers, the owner of the company recognizes a number of them as drug addicts, robbers, and even murderers. The owner says to the contractor, "I don't want those kinds of men working in my factory. I don't trust them. This is a place of morality, ethics, and responsibility. We are proud of our people and don't want a negative influence."

But the contractor responds, "Sir, you have always liked my work and trusted my judgment. Is that not true?"

"Yes," the owner replies.

"And you have never been dissatisfied with my work?"

"No, no, not at all."

"Then, you can rest assured; all will be as I have always performed. Every man with me, I certify. He is with me, and I speak for him no matter what he has done in the past. He is now my coworker and I guarantee him. He is 'in' my company."

This is what it means to be the righteousness of God. We are not in good standing with the "owner" because of our own goodness; we are in good standing with Him because of Christ's goodness. We are righteous "in Him."

WE ARE SANCTIFIED "IN CHRIST JESUS"

"To those who are sanctified in Christ Jesus" (1 Cor. 1:2). The word *sanctification* means to be "set apart as holy." Often we use it to refer to how much we have achieved in our walk with God. Unfortunately it has become a kind of spiritual thermometer, which often invites an improper understanding of the biblical meaning of the word. The word in 1 Corinthians 1 is past tense, indicating that "in Christ Jesus" sanctification is something that has already taken place and not something in progress. It is finished. God has made us holy in Christ. We are not partially "set apart" unto Christ but completely distinguished as His in every way from the moment that we came into Him.

The apostle Paul wrote, "But of Him you are in Christ Jesus, who became for us wisdom from God—and righteousness and sanctification and redemption—that, as it is written, 'He who glories, let him glory in the LORD'" (1 Cor. 1:30–31). Let's look carefully at these verses:

- *"But of Him you are in Christ Jesus."* It is God's work and God's act that united us in Christ.

- *"Who became for us wisdom from God."* When you feel short on wisdom, God says you can turn to Him, because all the wisdom you will ever need is "in Jesus." Of course, God often works through people to get that wisdom to us. That is why His body, the church, is so important.

- *"And righteousness and sanctification and redemption."* Jesus makes us righteous. He empowers us to live holy. As believers, we are righteous, holy, and redeemed "in Him." If we are ever tempted to glory in our own wisdom, righteousness, sanctification, or redemption, we are making a big mistake.

- *"He who glories, let him glory in the LORD."* If you think there is anything so good, so righteous, or so holy in you that you are entitled to boast of your accomplishments, you have missed the entire point of salvation by grace.

It is certainly true that we are in the process of becoming more like Jesus in our trek toward maturity. By fresh and new revelations from God's Word and by the help of the Holy Spirit we are brought to greater degrees of right living but not greater degrees of sanctification. That is a done deal. Both righteousness and sanctification are absolutes. We are not "partly" or "mostly" sanctified. The moment we were born again, we were set apart as holy to the Lord. Then from that moment until our dying day we are called by God to grow in holiness, with God's help and empowerment.

In Christ we are fully and completely set apart (Col. 2:9–10). It is within this completeness that we grow and mature. This gives us the liberty to live a life of joy in Jesus rather than constantly trying to do better for Him on our own.

WE ARE *NEW CREATURES* "IN CHRIST"

"Therefore, if anyone is in Christ, he is a new creation; old things have passed away; behold, all things have become new" (2 Cor. 5:17). We must not fall into the error of thinking that we are good enough, smart enough, or strong enough to make ourselves into new people. Such thinking only denies the deplorable situation of sin that was in us when we came into the world. "If we say that we have no sin, we deceive ourselves, and the truth is not in us. If we confess our sins, He is faithful and just to forgive us our sins and to cleanse us from all unrighteousness. If we say that we have not sinned, we make Him a liar, and His word is not in us" (1 John 1:8–10).

Remember, the work of Christ is to take care of our sin. If now "in Christ" we are made new, what were we before? We were:

- Dead in trespasses and sin (Eph. 2:1)
- Stranger and foreigners to God (Eph. 2:19)
- In league with the devil (John 8:44)
- In darkness (Eph. 5:8)
- Deceived (Titus 3:3)
- Without hope in the world (Eph. 2:12)
- Cursed (Gal. 3:10)
- Dominated by lust (Eph. 2:2)
- A child of wrath (Eph. 2:3)
- Alienated from God and hostile toward Him (Col. 1:21)
- Walking according to the course of this world (Eph. 2:2)

Praise God, when we are "in Christ" we are none of those things anymore!

WE ARE *BLESSED* WITH EVERY SPIRITUAL BLESSING

"Blessed be the God and Father of our Lord Jesus Christ, who has blessed us with every spiritual blessing in the heavenly places in Christ" (Eph. 1:3). Many who are unaware of what we have "in Christ" struggle greatly, feeling unworthy of God's attention and His blessings. And things such as unanswered prayer only add to the problem. Stop and think about this for a moment. The entire human race is in the same predicament, yet some people who are in Christ are still feeling condemned while others who are in Christ are experiencing His life.

The blessed life God desires is for all of us, not a select few. We all struggle to understand certain things. I have never met a person who continued to grow in Christ fail to eventually experience His grace and power. This is not because they discovered some new truth that showed them a better way to get to God, but because in time He personally came to them. None of us will ever rise high enough to touch God, but we can be assured that He will bend low enough to touch us and bring us up to Himself.

WE *REST FROM WORKS* WHEN "IN CHRIST"

"There remains therefore a rest for the people of God. For he who has entered His rest has himself also ceased from his works as God did from His" (Heb. 4:9–10). I have a friend who is obsessive compulsive. In fact, I am a little that way myself—actually, a lot that way because I can be bit of a perfectionist. When it comes to pleasing God, many Christians have a similar tendency. They believe we must be hard at work to please God. Some of us are willing to do anything to make sure God doesn't get angry with us. We feel our destiny is conditional based on our ability to perform. We base it on something that is happening within *ourselves*. Because we know we are "unfinished" in *ourselves*, we pursue personal perfection, forgetting that it is already ours *in Christ*.

When you feel you have to constantly reach up to God, failing to realize that He has already reached down to you, it is easy to believe that your salvation is established on how well you do in your efforts to please God. Perhaps you, like so many others, have felt the anxiety of wondering what you have failed to do to satisfy God, sometimes thinking day and night about such things.

Innate within mankind is the knowledge that we are separated from Him. This knowledge pushes us to try to get to Him *somehow*—by making up for the things we have done wrong, by showing Him that we are serious by the good things we do, or by denying ourselves somehow. The "rest" God promises us is not ceasing *to* work; it is ceasing *from* works. It is the recognition that there is nothing we can do to earn our salvation. It is realizing that salvation is a gift without attachments. It is free!

Do I work? Absolutely! But never with the idea that what I am doing is in some way a payment for my wrongdoing or an offering to show that I am truly sorry for my poor behavior. Confession and not penitence is what God requires. "If we confess our sins, He is faithful and just to forgive us our sins and to cleanse us from all unrighteousness" (1 John 1:9). If it seems that I have used this verse many times, I realize I have. It is because we must never forget that Christ's blood does indeed cleanse us from sin, all because of the blood of the cross.

A person does not work for his salvation because that work is already done. It is like Israel entering Canaan. It was said to be a land of rest. In it were fortified cities the Israelites did not build, houses full of good things they did not buy, wells they did not dig, olive orchards and vineyards they did not plant. Everything was already there for them (Deut. 6:10–11). In Christ we come into a grace we did not earn (Rom. 5:19), a sanctification we did not accomplish, and a righteousness that is not our own (Phil. 3:9; Rom. 3:21-22)—all because of the work of Jesus.

I love the words of this poem:

> Upon a life I did not live,
> Upon a death I did not die,
> Another's life, another's death,
> I stake my whole eternity.

Not on the tears which I have shed;
Not on the sorrows I have known,
Another's tears, another's griefs,
On them I rest, on them alone.

Not what these hands have done
Can save the guilty soul;
Not what this toiling flesh has borne
Can make the spirit whole.

Thy blood alone, Lord Jesus,
Can cleanse my soul from sin;
Thy Word alone, O Lamb of God,
Can give me peace within![4]

Jesus has dealt with all of my debts concerning sin. Now I am free to work as hard as I can in God's kingdom, not to appease Him but out of love and gratitude.

WE ARE NO LONGER *CONDEMNED* "IN CHRIST JESUS"

"There is therefore now no condemnation to those who are *in Christ Jesus*" (Rom. 8:1, emphasis added). Both my kids and grandkids have made mistakes. Some were pretty serious errors, but I have never condemned one of them. That is, I don't sentence them to doom, nor do I denounce, terrify, criticize, or yell at them. I do not shun or speak evil of them. Certainly I wished they had done better, but condemn? Not for a moment! Consequences? You bet, but only with the design to bring restoration and reconciliation. I did not lose an ounce of love for any of them. Think then of the person who is by nature love and can do a better job of loving than anyone who has ever lived. He is going to do a wonderful job of loving you and not condemning you when you turn to Him, no matter how embarrassed you are. The reason you are not condemned is because Jesus Himself is not condemnable, and so neither are you because you are "in Him."

WE ARE GOD'S *WORKMANSHIP*
CREATED "IN CHRIST JESUS"

"For we are His workmanship, created in Christ Jesus for good works, which God prepared beforehand that we should walk in them" (Eph. 2:10). Ever have someone behave in a way that embarrassed you and others present? It may have been at a party or another kind of gathering. Somebody, by his words or actions, showed little regard for others. What if all of God's work in us was for the purpose of preventing us from making fools of ourselves? What if holiness, righteousness, good living, purity, etc. were given to us so we could enjoy the party?

God's work in us is to remove anger, bitterness, unforgiveness, arrogance, and any other thing that brings death rather than life. Remember, God works in us to make changes, and He wants us to believe that those changes are real blessings. Romans 8:2 says, "For the law of the Spirit of life in Christ Jesus has made me free from the law of sin and death." This means there is no condemnation in Christ, but still we have His Spirit of life to help us live rightly. And He never stops working in us.

We can look back on every change God makes in us with deep appreciation, knowing it was greatly needed. I am amazed by the changes He has made in my life. The God I once horribly feared for what He expected and demanded of me has become the God I now invite to do His work and will in me in every way. And I am blessed daily by that work. It is good to not hate myself when I fail to live up to His standard. It is good to know I have someone who cares for me. The work He has done in my heart has produced good fruit that allows me to live joyfully "in Him."

WE ARE *PERFECT* "IN CHRIST JESUS"

"Him we preach, warning every man and teaching every man in all wisdom, that we may present every man perfect in Christ Jesus" (Col. 1:28). Only a perfect person can fellowship with a perfect God. But in ourselves we are imperfect. Now that Christ is our perfection, He brings us safely into God's presence. His perfection is our perfection: "By that will we have been sanctified through the offering of the body of Jesus Christ once for all.... For by one offering He has perfected forever those who are being sanctified" (Heb. 10:10, 14). As a result, we can experience the reality of 1 John 1:3: "That which we have seen and heard we declare to you, that you also may have fellowship with us; and truly our fellowship is with the Father and with His Son Jesus Christ."

WE ARE PART OF THE CHURCH "IN CHRIST"

"In whom the whole building, being fitted together, grows into a holy temple in the Lord, in whom you also are being built together for a dwelling place of God in the Spirit" (Eph. 2:21–22). You and I were made for community. If Satan wants to do anything, he wants to destroy relationships. That is why there are many people who feel lonely, abandoned, deserted, rejected, and isolated. They believe they are less than others and therefore consider themselves outsiders. They generally gravitate to people who feel the same way, and eventually they view themselves as a small group against the world.

Coming into Christ finds God saying, "You thought you were no good, that others were better than you. In the process you have become angry and bitter. This whole thing about Jesus is to let you know that I am as interested in you as in anyone else in the world." God won't have it any other way. He loves you no matter how you see it.

GOD'S FAVOR HAS BEEN POURED
OUT ON US "IN CHRIST"

"To the praise of the glory of His grace, by which He made us accepted in the Beloved" (Eph. 1:6). All the religions of the world except one find people reaching up to God attempting to please Him with their abilities, talents, polite actions, right living, and personal goodness. The exception is Christianity, where God reaches down to man. You didn't have to do a single thing to be loved by God. He made the effort to reach out to you despite your sinful condition. "God was in Christ reconciling the world to Himself, not imputing their trespasses to them, and has committed to us the word of reconciliation. Now then, we are ambassadors for Christ, as though God were pleading through us: we implore you on Christ's behalf, be reconciled to God" (2 Cor. 5:19–20).

Reconciliation is not something we create; God has already done it in Christ. Therefore act like a reconciled person. Certainly it is good to want to please Him but not because we think He may accept us better if we do good things. We are already accepted "in Christ."

WE HAVE OBTAINED AN *INHERITANCE* "IN CHRIST."

"In Him also we have obtained an inheritance, being predestined according to the purpose of Him who works all things according to the counsel of His will" (Eph. 1:11). If I had a rich relative, I wouldn't want him to die in order to obtain some of his riches. I'd rather he just gave some to me. God who owns everything and is not going to die wants to share what He owns with us. I can't fathom that, even though I believe it, so I'll just leave you to ponder that truth. As you do, consider these passages of Scripture:

> "But when the fullness of the time had come, God sent forth His Son, born of a woman, born under the law, to redeem those who were under the law, that we might receive the adoption as sons. And because you are sons, God has sent forth the Spirit of His Son into your hearts, crying out, "Abba, Father!" Therefore you are no longer a slave but a son, and if a son, then an heir of God through Christ.
>
> —Galatians 4:4–7

> Blessed be the God and Father of our Lord Jesus Christ, who according to His abundant mercy has begotten us again to a living hope through the resurrection of Jesus Christ from the dead, to an inheritance incorruptible and undefiled and that does not fade away, reserved in heaven for you, who are kept by the power of God through faith for salvation ready to be revealed in the last time.
>
> —1 Peter 1:3-5

> The Spirit Himself bears witness with our spirit that we are children of God, and if children, then heirs—heirs of God and joint heirs with Christ, if indeed we suffer with Him, that we may also be glorified together.
>
> —Romans 8:16-17

It amazes me that the God of all creation, who has always existed, would want me to be His constant companion forever. But it's true. That's the very reason He made you and me!

OUR FAITH IS "IN CHRIST JESUS"

"Knowing that a man is not justified by the works of the law but by faith in Jesus Christ, even we have believed in Christ Jesus, that we might be justified by faith in Christ and not by the works of the law; for by the works of the law no flesh shall be justified" (Gal. 2:16). In looking at the concept of faith, there are two kinds to keep in mind.

First, as far as our salvation is concerned, God wants us to exercise the kind of faith that "believes." This is the kind of faith Abraham had. He believed God, and it was credited to him as righteousness (Rom. 4:3). Yet we must note that Abraham's faith wasn't perfect; it needed to be strengthened: "He did not waver at the promise of God through unbelief, but was strengthened in faith, giving glory to God" (v. 20). So then there is faith that is already in us to be exercised by choice. It is a measure of faith. Using the little faith we have causes it to grow to greater measures of faith.

As Romans 1:17 says, "For in it [the gospel] the righteousness of God is revealed from faith to faith; as it is written, 'The just shall live by faith.'" This kind of faith was found in the woman who followed Jesus seeking healing for a menstrual condition that had caused her to bleed for twelve years. "And He said to her, 'Daughter, be of good cheer; your faith has made you well. Go in peace'" (Luke 8:48).

But there is yet another kind of faith that is not resident in us and needs to come through Jesus and by His Word. We can call it the gift of faith because it comes to us from outside of ourselves. A man whose son was demon possessed needed this kind of faith. Jesus told the man, "'If you can believe, all things are possible to him who believes.' Immediately the father of the child cried out and said with tears, 'Lord, I believe; help my unbelief!'" (Mark 9:23–24).

The Bible tells us there are those with no faith, as we read in Mark 4:40, "But He said to them, 'Why are you so fearful? How is it that you have no faith?'" But God in His favor and kindness gives faith to those who want it and need it. This is that second kind of faith, the faith that is "in" Him and not in us. I have a lot of faith in what God can do; that is, my faith directed toward Him, which is different from the faith Paul spoke of, which belongs to Jesus personally and that He exercises on our behalf or gives to us as a gift.[5]

The Bible tells us:

- *Faith comes by hearing God's Word:* "So then faith comes by hearing, and hearing by the word of God" (Rom. 10:17).

- *Faith comes from Jesus:* "Looking unto Jesus, the author and finisher of our faith" (Heb. 12:2); "To those who have obtained like precious faith with us by the righteousness of our God and Savior Jesus Christ" (2 Pet. 1:1).

WE HAVE THE *PROMISE OF LIFE* "IN CHRIST JESUS"

"Paul, an apostle of Jesus Christ by the will of God, according to the promise of life which is in Christ Jesus" (2 Tim. 1:1); "He who has the Son has life" (1 John 5:12). If a person has no notion about life other than the natural life we live right now, then the idea of eternal life will be hard to grasp. Eternal life is God's life. It is not subject to the condition of the human body. It is not bound by health, nor is it constrained by time, and it has no end.

Because you are in Christ, this amazing life has already come to live in you. That means that since Jesus is free from the things that bind us on earth, so are you free. Why? Because "the law of the Spirit of life in Christ Jesus has made me free from the law of sin and death" (Rom. 8:2). And because "you died, and your life is hidden with Christ in God. When Christ who is our life appears, then you also will appear with Him in glory" (Col. 3:3–4).

In a sense, when we were young, we were hidden in our parents. There we were given everything we needed to grow. The baby who can do absolutely nothing for himself is sheltered by caring parents. This is another picture of what it means to be in Christ. We are sheltered by Him and are dependent on Him for everything we need.

WE HAVE GOD'S *PURPOSE AND GRACE* "IN CHRIST JESUS"

"Who has saved us and called us with a holy calling, not according to our works, but according to His own purpose and grace which was given to us in Christ Jesus before time began" (2 Tim. 1:9). God has a purpose—an ultimate intention—for you and me. Make no mistake: He is actively working to bring that intention to pass at this very moment. He sees everything that happens to you. He sees because He is watching carefully and lovingly as He works to accomplish His purposes in and through you.

WE HAVE *LOVE* "IN CHRIST JESUS"

"Hold fast the pattern of sound words which you have heard from me, in faith and love which are in Christ Jesus" (2 Tim. 1:13). God's essence is love. I wish I could grasp that a bit better. In some ways I think I can because I have met some people who exemplified the love of God in profound ways. My grandmother is one example. The fragrance of love marked her life, and she was wonderful to be around. This is true of God. When we get beyond our misconceptions about who God really is, we are attracted by His unmistakable perfume—His love.

WE HAVE *GRACE* "IN CHRIST JESUS"

"You therefore, my son, be strong in the grace that is in Christ Jesus" (2 Tim. 2:1). My favorite definition of the word *grace* paints the idea of adding elegance to something.[6] That is a bit different from the subjective "favor or goodwill."[7] I think both are correct, but I like to think that God not only sees me favorably, but He also adds elegance to my life. No matter what you think of your life right now, God thinks you are elegant.

WE HAVE THE *TRUTH* "IN CHRIST"

"I am speaking the truth in Christ and not lying" (1 Tim. 2:7). We generally think of truth as the opposite of a falsehood or a lie. This is true, but God's Word also looks at it in another way. God sees truth not only as a thing but as an essence. He sees it as the nature of something. In this case, it is the nature of Jesus.

Nothing in the nature of Christ personifies or embodies evil. God does not have to try to be good, because that is who He is. He does not have to try to always tell the truth. He is truth. When we are in Christ, the same is true of you and me. I don't have to try to be good, because it is now in my nature to do what is right. That doesn't mean I am not tempted to turn from the truth; Jesus Himself was tempted. But because I am in Him, I have His Spirit to fight off other "natures." (See 2 Peter 1:2–4.)

"IN CHRIST" WE ARE ALL THE SAME

"There is neither Jew nor Greek, there is neither slave nor free, there is neither male nor female; for you are all one in Christ Jesus. And if you are Christ's, then you are Abraham's seed, and heirs according to the promise" (Gal. 3:28–29). As Christ's body, we are all one. But I can carry this beyond the realm of the church. In Christ I can love everyone and anyone—I can genuinely care about people no matter who they are. I can step across lines of color, social hindrances, educational obstacles, financial walls, and age barrier, because this is the example of Jesus.

I was talking with my friend Darrell Faxon about these benefits of being in Christ, and I love the way he sums up the truths we have explored in this chapter: "The good news is what Christ did for us—'that He was buried, and that He rose again the third day according to the Scriptures' (1 Cor. 15:4). The Scriptures say 'for us.' The good news is not about what God does with us. It is not about what God does through us. It is not about what God does in us. All those things are important, but they are not the gospel. According to the Scriptures, the gospel concerns the Son of God. Romans 1:4 says that the gospel that God promised through the prophets concerns His Son Jesus Christ. It isn't about us or what we have done. We are affected by it, but it is not about us. It is about Him. It is about what God did with and through and in Jesus Christ *for us*. It isn't about our activity or our work or our anything. It is about the activity and the work Jesus Christ did on our behalf."[8]

Amen.

CHAPTER 29

Christ "in Us" Is Our Only Hope

To them God willed to make known what are the
riches of the glory of this mystery among the Gentiles:
which is Christ in you, the hope of glory.

—COLOSSIANS 1:27

GOD STARTED HIS relationship with humanity in an intimacy of which we have only a glimpse. Marriage is perhaps one of the best illustrations of the divine plan. The whole idea of two becoming one in a way in which individual uniqueness is blended together seems to be God's plan for Himself and His creation. The design of our very nature—that we were crafted in His image and likeness—would certainly be a prerequisite for such a relationship.

But it often seems our understanding of this kind of closeness is intellectual, not personal; more like the kind of conclusion an archeologist might draw about an ancient building from examining bricks buried in the sand. Adam's sin has blurred our eyes from God's original intention. At best we perceive that something is missing in our lives. We know that we are not what we are supposed to be. Guilt and condemnation, loneliness and fear tell us that we are outside the original intention, so we search for ways to ease the pain.

Originally Adam walked with God without a single care. Worry and other forms of pain did not exist. Evil as we know it was not a part of his wonderful relationship with God. The two were so connected they could literally walk and talk together. But Adam was enticed to see what it would be like to live outside of this powerful relationship. "You can be like God," the devil coaxed. "You can make it on your own. Look who you are; you are a powerful person." Sadly Adam accepted the lie and in the process walked away from God. Soon after he felt the absence of his friend. And just as quickly he found that he was incapable of controlling the world he once ruled. He became his own god but incapable of ruling much of anything.

As a result, Adam lost sight of the meaning of life. He lost vision and purpose. He even lost his ability to perceive his own condition. Then he blamed both God and his wife for his problems (Gen. 3:12).

We are still trying to do the same today—claiming to be gods by thinking that we can make it on our own. At the same time our best efforts at making something out of life leave us feeling lonely and rejected. But we are determined to go on, and no matter how much God tries to tell us that we are not doing well, we still don't believe Him.

He introduced the Ten Commandments, and mankind immediately rebelled against them. The Law was not a bad thing. It was good in that it showed us our weaknesses and the folly of thinking that we could be good on our own. The Pharisees of Jesus's day insisted that they could be righteous by doing good deeds. They were proud of their ability to do good by keeping the Law. But Jesus exposed their error by showing their righteousness was only exterior. On the outside they had learned to look the part of a righteous person, but on the inside they were full of evil. (See Matthew 23:25, 27.)

No matter how hard God tries to tell us that we are not doing well, we either insist we are or contend that we will try harder next time. Yet the truth still remains, "There is none righteous, no, not one; there is none who understands; there is none who seeks after God. They have all turned aside; they have together become unprofitable; there is none who does good, no, not one" (Rom. 3:10–12).

These are not statements to condemn. They are simply facts of this present life. Jesus said, "For God did not send His

Son into the world to condemn the world, but that the world through Him might be saved" (John 3:17). As we have explored before, condemnation is not on God's mind (Rom. 8:1); the revelation of our condition is. If we don't know what's wrong, we will never be able to participate in the solution to fix it.

THE SOLUTION IS CHRIST "IN" US

In God's marvelous plan of salvation He has never had in mind that we were to become holy and righteous outside of His immediate help—a help wrought by the literal presence of God's Spirit dwelling in the human spirit, as the following scriptures declare (emphasis added):

> The Spirit of truth, whom the world cannot receive, because it neither sees Him nor knows Him; but you know Him, for *He dwells with you and will be in you.*
>
> —JOHN 14:17

> But you are not in the flesh but in the Spirit, if *indeed the Spirit of God dwells in you.* Now if anyone does not have the Spirit of Christ, he is not His.
>
> —ROMANS 8:9

> I have been crucified with Christ; it is no longer I who live, but *Christ lives in me*; and the life which I now live in the flesh I live by faith in the Son of God, who loved me and gave Himself for me.
>
> —GALATIANS 2:20

> And because you are sons, *God has sent forth the Spirit of His Son into your hearts*, crying out, "Abba, Father!"
>
> —GALATIANS 4:6

> For it is *God who works in you* both to will and to do for His good pleasure.
>
> —PHILIPPIANS 2:13

> To them God willed to make known what are the riches
> of the glory of this mystery among the Gentiles: which is
> *Christ in you*, the hope of glory.
>
> —COLOSSIANS 1:27

An open heart to Jesus allows Him access into the deepest part of our being. Here fellowship fuses a person into a unique relationship with God. It is Christ's blood that makes us new in Him. Perhaps huge volumes could be written about the blood of Jesus. But if you remember only a few things about Jesus's blood, remember these:

- It reconciles us to God.
- It gives access into God's presence.
- It frees us from guilt and condemnation.
- It washes us from sin.
- It guarantees eternal life.
- It sanctifies us from the world.
- It's a weapon against the enemy of our soul. (See Revelation 12:11.)

Our amazing salvation is wrapped up in Jesus. That is without question. Without Him there would be no way of being reconciled to God, and we would be without God forever. But that is not the final story. As Christ's representatives in the earth, our mission is to proclaim God's glory. When we walk in the freedom we have in Christ and share the good news of the gospel, we reveal God's heart for mankind. And the world is in desperate need of understanding the Father's great love for all of us.

Our world is filled with people who have no idea what real love is. They yearn for it but never find it. Our world is ready for the Father's love. People need the assurance that someone cares, that there is a real God with real compassion—someone who is truly a Father.

Look carefully at everything Jesus says about His mission, and it all ends in obedience, honor, love, and worship of the Father. In my early years of Christianity much of the emphasis in the church was on holiness. Later it was the Holy Spirit. After that it was, "It's all about Jesus" and "What would Jesus do?" Now the groundswell is the Father. These were all areas God wanted highlighted as He revealed Himself to the world. Most of us have not had much of a revelation of the Father. So I want to close with some of the most outstanding revelations of the Father as testified by Jesus:

> Then Jesus answered and said to them, "Most assuredly, I say to you, the Son can do nothing of Himself, but what He sees the Father do; for whatever He does, the Son also does in like manner."
>
> —John 5:19

> I can of Myself do nothing. As I hear, I judge; and My judgment is righteous, because I do not seek My own will but the will of the Father who sent Me.
>
> —John 5:30

> Just what I have been saying to you from the beginning. I have many things to say and to judge concerning you, but He who sent Me is true; and I speak to the world those things which I heard from Him.
>
> —John 8:25–26

> When you lift up the Son of Man, then you will know that I am He, and that I do nothing of Myself; but as My Father taught Me, I speak these things. And He who sent Me is with Me. The Father has not left Me alone, for I always do those things that please Him.
>
> —John 8:28–29

> I must work the works of Him who sent Me while it is day.
>
> —John 9:4

Therefore My Father loves Me, because I lay down My life that I may take it again. No one takes it from Me, but I lay it down of Myself. I have power to lay it down, and I have power to take it again. This command I have received from My Father.

—John 10:17–18

Father, I desire that they also whom You gave Me may be with Me where I am, that they may behold My glory which You have given Me; for You loved Me before the foundation of the world. O righteous Father! The world has not known You, but I have known You; and these have known that You sent Me. And I have declared to them Your name, and will declare it, that the love with which You loved Me may be in them, and I in them.

—John 17:24–26

Two powerful truths sum up most of what has been discussed in the pages of this book. First, *we are in a blood covenant relationship with Jesus.* As a result, we are no longer under the control of the enemy. When Satan's demons try to tell you that you still belong to them, tell them to check the record. Tell them that by blood covenant you are related to Jesus and that your name is written in the Lamb's Book of Life.

The second truth is this: *we are freed from sin by the blood of Jesus.* This means that when the enemy brings to mind past sin, creating condemnation and guilt, tell him, "Yes, I'm guilty, but someone has substituted His life for mine. I've talked my sin over with Him, and He has let me know that He has personally paid my debt. *Now nobody can touch the baby—and I'm the baby.*"

Notes

BOOK EPIGRAPH

1. "There Is a Fountain" by William Cowper. Public domain.

CHAPTER 1: A COVENANT OF BLOOD

1. Dwight L. Moody preached this in a sermon at the Free Church Assembly Hall, Edinburgh, Scotland, on December 9, 1873.

2. Darrel Faxon in personal communication with the author. Used with permission.

3. Rosalie Marie Levy, *Heavenly Friends* (Boston: St. Paul Editions, 1984).

4. John Wesley, "Salvation by Faith," preached at St. Mary's, Oxford University, June 18, 1738, http://new.gbgm-umc.org/umhistory/wesley/sermons/1/ (accessed November 7, 2013).

5. Shira Sorko-Ram writes in *I Became as a Jew* (Dallas: Maoz, Inc., 1991) that "one of the greatest blind spots in Rabbinical Judaism is in regard to the blood atonement. Perhaps this lack of understanding came about as Jewish religious leaders over the years attempted to distance themselves from Christian doctrine. But at the time of Yeshua (Jesus), the Jews certainly understood and practiced blood sacrifice."

6. Harold S. Kushner, *To Life!* (Boston: Warner Books, 1993), 24.

7. There are those who claim God dealt differently with peoples of different dispensations. C. I. Scofield divided these dispensations, or ages of time, into seven distinct periods: 1) Innocence (creation to Adam's fall), 2) Conscience (Adam's fall to Noah), 3) Government (Noah to Abraham), 4) Promise (Abraham to Moses), 5) Law (Moses to Christ), 6) Grace (the church age), and 7) the Kingdom (the millennium). The theory is untenable if by it anyone suggests that the manner God uses for relational covenant making changes from dispensation to dispensation. This work attempts to show that the entire Bible fits into a covenant framework rather than the idea that covenants served only for a particular reason within a certain time period. Even though there are decided differences between *dispensational* time periods, their similarities must not be ignored. Certainly it should be noted that the different ages of human history up to the birth of Christ gave progressive degrees of spiritual revelation, each unfolding and revealing a little more of

213

God's personality as well as of His plan of salvation, a plan eventually to be fulfilled in Jesus.

8. Passover was indeed a remembrance, but Communion is much more. According to 1 Corinthians 10:16 it is a communion, a fellowship, and a participation (Greek *koinonia*) in the body and blood of Christ. There is in the new covenant of grace something available to those in relationship with God that was not available to those under the old covenant Law.

9. Paul E. Billheimer, *Destined for the Throne* (Fort Washington, PA: Christian Literature Crusade, 1975), 23.

10. Ibid., 49.

CHAPTER 2: LIFE IS IN THE BLOOD

1. WebMD.com, "How the Heart Works," http://www.webmd.com/heart -disease/guide/how-heart-works (accessed December 13, 2013).

2. Shirley A. Riggs, "Blood," *Grolier Multimedia Encyclopedia*, Grolier Online, http://gme.grolier.com/article?assetid=0036010-0 (accessed December 13, 2013).

CHAPTER 3: THE SOURCE OF LIFE AND PEACE

1. Centers for Disease Control and Prevention, "United States Life Tables, 2008" *National Vital Statistics Report* 61, no. 3, http://www.cdc .gov/nchs/data/nvsr/nvsr61/nvsr61_03.pdf (accessed November 8, 2013).

2. In his book *The Chemistry of the Blood* Dr. M. R. DeHaan has proposed that the mother of a child does not pass sin to her children, as does the father because normally the mother's blood never comes in contact with the blood of her child. Only when the sperm enters the ovum does blood begin to appear. "It is unnecessary that a single drop of blood be given to the developing embryo in the womb of the mother. Such is the case according to scientists. The mother provides the fetus (the unborn developing infant) with the nutritive elements for the building of that little body in the secret of her womb, but all the blood which forms in it is formed in the embryo itself. From the time of conception to the time of birth of the infant not ONE SINGLE DROP OF BLOOD ever passes from mother to child. The placenta, that mass of temporary tissue known better as 'afterbirth,' forming the link between mother and child, is so constructed that although all the soluble nutritive elements such as proteins, fats, carbohydrates, salts, minerals and even antibodies pass freely from mother to child and the waste products of the child's metabolism are passed back to the mother's circulation, no actual interchange of a single drop of blood ever occurs normally. All the blood which is in that child is produced within the child itself. The

mother contributes no blood at all." (M. R. DeHaan, *The Chemistry of Blood* [Grand Rapids, MI: Zondervan, 1943], 31).

Not everyone agrees with DeHaan. In the notes of the book *Written in Blood* Robert E. Coleman writes, "Some contend that because of His virgin conception Christ did not actually have human blood. The idea comes from the belief that the blood of a human body is formed in the fetus itself by the introduction of the male sperm, and therefore has no direct contact with the mother's body. According to this view the mother supplies the developing infant with the nutritive elements for the building of the body, but there is no actual interchange of blood between the child and the mother. If this is the case, then the blood in the physical body of Christ would be uniquely the very blood of God, while only His flesh was human. This position has been popularized by Dr. M. R. DeHaan in his stimulating book, *The Chemistry of the Blood*.... To support his view, Dr. DeHaan quotes from several recognized medical authorities. Without trying to discredit this position, I think that it is only fair to note that other medical doctors seriously question its validity. However, regardless of the biological nature of the situation, I see no reason why it should be an issue. The fact that God conceived Jesus would itself rule out the hereditary transmission of sin. I am inclined to believe that His human nature included both His flesh and blood, and both were equally free of any moral corruption." (Robert E. Coleman, *Written in Blood* [Old Tappan, New Jersey: Fleming Revell, 1972], 19–20.)

There is yet another point to consider, presented by my friend Rick Kline: "I think DeHaan misses the point and makes the 'blood line' the issue without considering the following: How can it be said that Mary did not pass on the 'sin nature' to Jesus, yet Joseph would have if his sperm was used to impregnate Mary? Doesn't this imply seminal (semen) guilt? Wasn't Mary's father a sinner with a sin nature? Since Mary's physical characteristics (including her eggs) are the result of the union of Mary's father, who had a sin nature, and Mary's mother who also had a sin nature, how can we say Mary's egg was void of sin nature? If we think that Mary's egg was not tainted with the sin nature, then we would have to conclude that no other aspect of Mary's constitution had the sin nature either. It's all or none." (In communication with the author; used with permission.)

One more point is fitting. It comes from my friend Jim Ayars: "About original sin. The problem with most theories about how it is 'transmitted' is that they deal with humanity as individual persons, rather than corporately as humanity. When Adam, the head of the human race, fell, all humanity fell with him. Thus human nature— humanity—was corrupted at its source. SIN is a spiritual virus which infected all humanity from Adam to the present. In the biblical sense we all were 'in Adam' when he fell. God has replaced Adam with His own Son as the head of the human race. Now 'in Christ' we have been made alive. We are sinless, righteous, victorious, complete IN HIM. Christ retraced the steps that Adam should have taken, and was victorious where Adam failed. We, in Him, share in, partake of, Christ's victory." Jim also notes: "About the sinful human nature and the deity of Christ—SIN (as a spiritual virus, which indwells humanity) cannot exist in the immediate presence of deity. The incarnation automatically destroys whatever sin resides in humanity. In that way Christ was totally 'without sin' in His humanity." (In personal communication with the author. Used with permission.)

I give you the four ideas listed above to stimulate interest. In reality only God knows how all of this goes together to produce in Jesus (who is God) a human body, yet one without sin.

3. Andrew Murray, *The Blood of the Cross* (New Kensington, PA: Whitaker House, 1981), 13.

4. Billheimer, *Destined for the Throne*, 35–36.

5. Dutch Sheets, *Intercessory Prayer* (Ventura, CA: Regal Books, 1996), 200.

6. Murray, *The Blood of the Cross*, 145.

CHAPTER 4: RELATIONSHIP BY AGREEMENT

1. Arthur W. Pink, *The Divine Covenants* (Grand Rapids, MI: Baker Books, 1973), 11.

2. Leon Morris, *The Apostolic Preaching of the Cross*, third edition (Grand Rapids, MI: Wm. B. Eerdmans Publishing Co., 1965), 78–79.

3. Billheimer, *Destined for the Throne*, 25.

4. In the *Theological Dictionary of the Old Testament*, vol. 2, M. Weinfeld says, "The original meaning of the Hebrew *brith* is not 'agreement or settlement between two partners' as is commonly argued. *Brith* implies, first and foremost the notion of 'imposition,' 'liability,' or 'obligation'...thus we find that *brith* is commanded, which certainly cannot be said about mutual agreement" (Grand Rapids, MI: William B. Eerdmans, 1975, 253–255.) Weinfeld's conclusion is highly questionable. To say that covenant is commanded because of the words "imposition," "liability," and "obligation" does not take into account that these same words also apply to virtually any mutual agreement. If a person sets his hand to a contract, whether willingly or unwillingly, he is imposed upon and encumbers himself with liability and obligation, and cannot get out of that encumbrance without severe penalty.

5. C. S. Lewis, *Mere Christianity* (New York: HarperCollins, 1980), 49.

6. Interestingly some Rabbinic Jewish scholars argue that the Old Testament system of sacrificing animals was something the ancient Hebrews picked up from surrounding heathen nations. Missionary Shira Sorko-Ram, author of *I Became as a Jew*, writes that some teachers within Rabbinic Judaism "explain that Moses, knowing that it was very hard to change everything at once, indulged his people by letting them sacrifice animals. But as far as God is concerned, the rabbis claim, blood sacrifice has no significance" (page 27). On the contrary, we know from Scripture that God instituted the sacrificial system to point to Jesus as the sacrifice for human sin.

7. Meredith G. Kline, *Treaty of the Great King: The Covenant Structure of Deuteronomy* (Eugene, OR: Wipf and Stock Publishers, 2012).

8. The Abrahamic covenant is often called the covenant of promise whereas the Mosaic covenant is called the covenant of works. If promise (Abraham) is the primary aspect of covenant-making, then we must conclude covenants with God are covenants of grace. But if it were only by grace, then breaking it would not require God to make judgment upon it. If, however, the covenant is an agreement, then it seems it must be of works. But if it is of works, how do we reconcile the element of grace based on "for by grace you are saved"? Abraham's covenant of "promise" certainly seems to fit into the category of grace, whereas Moses's "agreement" with God appears to fit into the idea of works. Do they, then, represent aspects of different covenants, or is God sharing with us different aspects of the same covenant? If they are different, which one fits where? Under which one do we function today? If covenants that God makes with mankind are different at different times in history, we lose perspective on a model. We have long believed that the New Testament was mirrored in the Old. But the image becomes blurred if we cannot find some consistency by which God deals with people in both the Old and New Testaments. The solution seems to be in integrating the two concepts, promise and agreement, into aspects of the same covenant relationship. It appears that the grace of God is what extends the opportunity to join Him in agreement in the first place. Grace is God reaching out to man. It does not arbitrarily wipe out responsibility in the relationship or the consequences involved if the covenant is broken. We are still accountable to the stipulations of the agreement. There are things that must be done in order to keep the agreement alive. And there is a price to be paid for failing the contract. This is in line with the words of James when he says, "Show me your faith without works, and I will show you my faith by my works" (James 2:18). One covenant shows us grace that brings salvation, the other shows us responsibility in the relationship.

9. George Ricker Berry, "Covenant: Between God and Men," in James Orr, gen. ed., *The International Standard Bible Encyclopedia*, vol. 2 (Grand Rapids, MI: William B. Eerdmans Publishing Co. 1939), 728.

10. Donald K. Campbell, *Daniel: Decoder of Dreams* (n.p.: Victor Books, 1979), 49.

CHAPTER 5: SEALED IN BLOOD

1. H. Clay Trumbull, *The Blood Covenant* (New York: Charles Scribner's Sons, 1885), 38. Viewed online at Google Books.

2. In his book *Covenant: The History of a Biblical Idea* Delbert R. Hillers affirms the idea that ancient covenants were first "made" in blood and then, if failed, "paid" for in blood. He writes, "An ancient treaty, then, is essentially an elaborate oath. There are two fundamental components: the thing to be performed, and the oath, the invoking of divine vengeance in case the promise is not kept. These basic features are discernibly present in extremely early texts, even though the documents are in part obscure or damaged." (Baltimore, MD: The Johns Hopkins University Press, 1969, 28.)

3. H. Clay Trumbull well understood the concept of sharing lives through blood covenants. He wrote: "The blood is the life; the heart as the fountain of blood is the fountain of life; both blood and heart are sacred to the Author of life. The possession, or the gift, of the heart or of the blood, is the possession, or the gift, of the very nature of its primal owner. That has been the world's thought in all the ages....The belief seems to have been universal, not only that the blood is the life of the organism in which it originally flows, but that in its transfer from one organism to another the blood retains its life, and so carries with it a vivifying power. There are traces of this belief in the earliest legends of the Old World, and of the New; in classic story; and in medical practices as well, all the world over, from time immemorial until the present day." (*The Blood Covenant*, 110.).

4. Ibid., 57.

5. David Livingstone, *Missionary Travels and Researches in South Africa*, http://www.gutenberg.org/files/1039/1039-h/1039-h.htm (accessed November 11, 2013).

6. Ibid.

7. Henry W. Little, *Henry M. Stanley: His Life, Travels, and Explorations* (Philadelphia, PA: J.B. Lippincott, Company, 1890), 198; http://archive.org/stream/henrymstanleyhis00littrich#page/n3/mode/2up (accessed December 20, 2013).

8. Trumbull, *The Blood Covenant*, 5.

9. Don Richardson, *Peace Child* (Ventura, CA: Regal Books, 1975).

CHAPTER 6: THE OLD TESTAMENT BLOOD COVENANT

1. The *NIV Study Bible* claims the Abrahamic covenant came in two parts, A and B. Part A is said to be a "Royal (land) Grant" type of covenant. Part B is said to be a "Suzerain-vassal" type covenant. Part A was "made with 'righteous' (his faith was 'credited...to him as righteousness,' v. 6) Abram (and his descendants, v. 16)." It was "an unconditional divine promise to fulfill the grant of the land; a self-maledictory oath symbolically enacted it (v. 17)." Part B was "made with Abraham as patriarchal head of his household." It was "a conditional divine pledge to be Abraham's God and the God of his descendants (cf. 'as for me,' v. 4; 'as for you,' v. 9); the condition: total consecration to the Lord as symbolized by circumcision.)" (*NIV Study Bible* [Grand Rapids, MI: Zondervan, 1985, 1995, 2002, 2008, 2011].) Certainly there were two parts to the Abrahamic covenant, but not quite the way the *NIV Study Bible* explains it. Their explanation makes it appear that two different agreements make up the sum of the covenant; rather, God ratified the agreement in Genesis 15, and Abraham ratified it in Genesis 17. In Nehemiah 9:8 the Levites spoke of "a covenant," singular, that God made with Abraham.

2. Again, did God have two covenants with Abraham, or just one? If He had but one, then the account of the covenant in Genesis 15 and the account in Genesis 17 must be parts of the same agreement. If this is true, then the part in Genesis 15 is God's signature on the agreement, and the part in Genesis 17 is Abraham's.

   Some do not see the two parts to the one agreement: God's part in Genesis 15:9–18 and Abraham's part in Genesis 17:1–14. Without putting the two together to get a full "cutting of the covenant," making it a complete "blood covenant," it is easy to take the first half and come up with an "unconditional covenant." In this case Abraham has nothing to say in the matter. Serious problems concerning choice and free will result when men are seen as objects of covenants with God and are not fully recognized as participants in the agreements.

   If it were true that God's covenants with mankind were unilateral, history would be redundant and unnecessary. It would have no meaning. God could have sat Adam and Eve down, after they sinned, and said, "This is the way it is going to be; you will no longer do what I tell you not to do. It will never happen again."

   There is, however, a bit of a problem in arguing too heavily for "mutuality" in agreements with God, which, for the most part, this book does. The problem is that within the Abrahamic covenant there is an "unconditional promise," basically given to all humanity. And how do you make an unconditional promise to all of humanity through a person who has to mutually agree to certain stipulations? This "promise" within the agreement is not only seen as the permanent establishment of the Jewish people, but also as the promise of the Messiah who would offer salvation to all mankind. This surely was an unconditional promise, for no man by any act of disobedience could stop it. Generally when one party breaks a mutual agreement, it is nullified so that the other party no longer has any obligations. (See chapter 27, "The Covenant of Promise.") The whole agreement shuts down when one of the parties breaks it. Eventually both Abraham and his people broke the covenant. This is evidenced by the need for sacrifices offered as atonement for sin. But the promise was not nullified because of sin. This part of the agreement continued in affect.

On the other hand, in arguing that mutuality was the basis for the contract, we note that Abraham had to freely consent to the relationship. It was not forced upon him. In this sense it is difficult to legitimately call the Abrahamic covenant an "unconditional covenant."

One of the primary ways scholars try to determine the kind and type of covenants God makes with mankind, and the manner in which they are made, is to study other covenants of the Near East. However, in doing so we must consider the possibility that these earthly agreements were distortions of the divine, or that they are unique creations of mankind by themselves. It is dangerous to assume that the water downstream is as pure as that of its source.

The *NIV Study Bible* gives the following as names and descriptions of covenants and treaties in the ancient Near East.

"**Royal Grant (unconditional)** A king's grant (of land or some other benefit) to a loyal servant for faithful or exceptional service. The grant was normally perpetual and unconditional, but the servant's heirs benefited from it only as they continued their father's loyalty and service. (Cf. 1 Sa 8:14; 22:7; 27:6; Est 8:1.)"

"**Parity** A covenant between equals, binding them to mutual friendship or at least to mutual respect for each other's spheres and interests. Participants called each other 'brother.' (Cf. Ge 21:27; 26:31; 31:44–54; 1 Ki 5:12; 15:19: 20:32–34; Am 1:9.)"

"**Suzerain-vassal (conditional)** A covenant regulating the relationship between a great king and one of his subject kings. The great king claimed absolute right of sovereignty, demanded total loyalty and service (the vassal must 'love' his suzerain) and pledged protection of the subject's realm and dynasty, conditional on the vassal's faithfulness and loyalty to him. The vassal pledged absolute loyalty to his suzerain—whatever service his suzerain demanded—and exclusive reliance on the suzerain's protection. Participants called each other 'lord' and 'servant' or 'father' and 'son.' (Cf. Jos 9:6, 8; Eze 17:13–18; Hos 12:1.)"

3. In Jeremiah 34:18–20 nothing is said of circumcision during the formation of a covenant when Israel passed between the bloody halves of an animal cut in two pieces. Despite the procedure used in this case, circumcision still stands as God's method of ratifying an agreement. It appears that this passage is mentioned not so much to identify a method for signing a covenant, but to warn the people against violating blood covenanting in general. Notice that the words *circumcision* and *uncircumcision* are both mentioned earlier in Jeremiah 9:25-26, leading us to believe that during this time in history these people still understood that circumcision was necessary as a "sign" for covenant relationship with God.

CHAPTER 7: THE RULES OF THE AGREEMENT

1. Rick Kline in personal communication with the author. Used with permission.

2. Kushner, *To Life!*, 25.

3. Some believe that in the first two chapters of Genesis God set forth a covenant called the Edenic covenant. It might have contained the original stipulations for Adam to have dominion of Planet Earth (Gen. 2:16–17). A second covenant called the Adamic covenant is thought to have been established after Adam sinned. The conditions of this covenant are said to be, in part: 1) curse upon the serpent and the serpent's influencer, Satan; 2) pain in childbirth; 3) woman subject to her husband; and 4) the ground cursed. However, what may appear to be provisions for a covenant are really the results of a failed one. The four points are not stipulations of a covenant but the devastating results of a broken agreement (Gen. 3:14, 16–17). Curses, condemnation, and judgment only follow the breaking of an established contract; they are not what put it into effect. Therefore we must assume that a covenant relationship existed from the very beginning. It is highly possible that God did, indeed, re-covenant with Adam after he sinned. But the curses from the previously failed agreement must not be thought to be the stipulations of the new contract.

4. The Greeks referred to the Ten Commandments as the Decalogue. Merrill Unger says, "The Ten Commandments are a statement of the terms of the covenant God made with His chosen people; and in this respect they are to be distinguished from the elaborate system of law known as the Mosaic. The vast legal system of Israel, civil, criminal, judicial, and ecclesiastical, was framed after the covenant law, not with a view of expanding it, but to enforce it.... Its chief object was to secure

through the instrumentality of the magistrate, that if the proper love should fail to influence the hearts and lives of the people, still the right should be maintained. The elaborate system was designed as an educator, to lead the people into the great principles of life embodied in the Ten Commandments and afterward exhibited in Christ. The Mosaic system was only a temporary expedient to achieve a given end, whereas the Ten Commandments are a statement of principles to continue for all time." (Merrill F. Unger, *The New Unger's Bible Dictionary* [Chicago: Moody Publishers, 2006], 1267).

This means that when the law was abolished (Eph. 2:15), the principles were not. The law of Christ is the new embodiment of the principles of the Ten Commandments. That's why Christ "in us" forms a new administration in which the motives for righteousness come from within. It's important to understand that the Ten Commandments stood to tell mankind what to do without giving any help in doing them. It was expectation without joyful motivation. It was administered from an external source—tablets of stone. The new law in Christ works from within and gives a personal desire to fulfill righteousness from an internal source—laws written upon the fleshly tablets of the human heart. This does not mean that originally men did not have consciences; they simply had not been given the Holy Spirit as a helper.

5. Kushner, *To Life!*, 22.

CHAPTER 8: THE "SIGN" OF THE AGREEMENT

1. Romans 4:9–12 makes it clear that physical circumcision does not save a person. Abraham believed God; his relationship with God was based on his faith in God (James 2:23). Later, however, God wanted to secure their relationship in a binding manner through the act of physical circumcision. As I have previously stated, the sign God requires of us under the new covenant is a circumcision of the heart. Since Abraham's salvation came from his faith before he was circumcised, God may have required this sign of circumcision to enable Abraham to always remember the covenant. It may also have been used as a testimony to the world, to tell them whose side he was on.

2. Corporate identity in Christ is the basis for salvation. However, salvation is also an individual matter between a person and God and determined only through Jesus (Acts 4:12). People born in Christian homes, and in nations that are largely Christian, sometimes feel they have a birthright that assures them a relationship with God. Judaism follows a similar line of thinking. Jewish nationalism builds a powerfully unified people but diminishes the recognition for personal responsibility before God. D. A. Carson, Douglas J. Moo, and Leon Morris explain the concept:

"In the past, it is argued, most Christian scholars assumed that Paul was dealing with legalistic Jews who counted up their good works in order to get into heaven. But many modern scholars are convinced that first-century Judaism was nothing like this. While this case has been argued in the past, E. P. Sanders's 1977 monograph *Paul and Palestinian Judaism* is the touchstone for the contemporary discussion. The heart of Sanders's argument is that the Judaism Paul knew was not a religion in which works were the means of becoming saved, or justified. Rather, in a pattern Sanders calls 'covenantal nomism,' first-century Jews believed that they were saved by means of their corporate election as a covenant people. Works or obedience to the law in this scheme does not save the Jew but maintains his or her status in the saving covenant relationship. If Paul's Jewish opponents were covenantal nomists rather than legalists, quite a different picture of Paul's teaching on fundamental issues such as justification and the law emerges. In fact, contemporary scholarship witnesses several different, and sometimes mutually exclusive, pictures of Paul's teaching about this covenantal nomism. And since the book of Romans from beginning to end contains teaching about justification, Jews, and the law, these revised pictures of Paul are evident in many recent studies of Romans." (D. A. Carson, Douglas J. Moo, and Leon Morris, *An Introduction to the New Testament* [Grand Rapids, MI: Zondervan, 1992], 252.)

In the *Biblical Archeology Review*, Nov/Dec 1994, 110–115, there were three articles describing a Dead Sea Scroll entitled, *Miqsat Ma'ase Ha-Torah* (MMT), which is translated "The Works of the Law." The material demonstrates what Sanders said in 1977 regarding the function of the Law according to the ancient view of the Jews in the time of Paul. Sanders did not have this information when he wrote, but the MMT later confirmed Sander's assessment.

3. Unlike the Christian view that a person enters into covenant with God only on the basis of a conscious decision to accept Jesus, the Jew believes that he is born into a relationship with God. Harold Kushner explains this view: "A Jew is born into the Covenant with God whether he wants to be or not, and this Covenant involves pain and sacrifice as well as honor and sanctity" (Kushner, *To Life!*, 232–233).

CHAPTER 9: CIRCUMCISION OF THE FLESH

1. Information on circumcision from *Funk & Wagnalls New Encyclopedia*, vol. 6 (Chicago: Funk & Wagnalls, n.d.), 298–299.

2. Merrill C. Farley, gen. ed. *The Zondervan Pictorial Encyclopedia of the Bible*, vol. 1, A–C (Grand Rapids, MI: Zondervan, 1975), 867.

3. Kushner, *To Life!*, 232.

4. There is the thought that ancient treaties differed considerably from ancient law. Supposedly treaties were formulated in such a way so as to cover entire families. Not only was the person signing the agreement responsible for keeping it, but also his entire household held equal accountability. Should he fail to live up to the contract, he, along with his family, all paid the price. The power of the treaty was the strength of the curse associated with it, and the curse affected everything about the person, including his family. Ancient law, on the other hand, demanded a person pay only for his own crime. He was to pay in proportion to the damage done—eye for eye and tooth for tooth. "You are great in counsel and mighty in work, for your eyes are open to all the ways of the sons of men, to give everyone according to his ways and according to the fruit of his doings" (Jer. 32:19). However, these two concepts should not be looked upon as having different roots. Both are seen under Moses in the Old Testament contract. Moses is the initial signer, circumcision being the sign of the signature on the agreement. But in order for divine protection and blessing to be extended to his household, his wife and children also had to enter into the agreement. Therefore every male had to be circumcised. Every person had to sign the divine treaty to be protected and blessed by God. At the same time every person paid for his own sin. The Law made it clear that each person was to give a personal account of his actions. The Law amounted to the stipulations within the agreement.

CHAPTER 10: CIRCUMCISION OF THE HEART

1. It is important to know the Scriptures that lead to salvation: *recognize the need:* "For all have sinned and fall short of the glory of God" (Rom. 3:23); *repent:* "I tell you, no; but unless you repent you will all likewise perish" (Luke 13:3); *receive Jesus:* "But as many as received Him, to them He gave the right to become children of God, to those who believe in His name" (John 1:12); and *confess Jesus:* "If you confess with your mouth the Lord Jesus and believe in your heart that God has raised Him from the dead, you will be saved. For with the heart one believes unto righteousness, and with the mouth confession is made unto salvation" (Rom. 10:9–10).

2. Ewald M. Plass, *What Luther Says* (St. Louis: Concordia Publishing House, 1959), 321.

CHAPTER 11: GOD'S REDEMPTION PLAN

1. This beautiful story of Ruth and Boaz gives us a unique picture of the redemptive work of Jesus. Boaz develops a cordial relationship with Ruth, perhaps even falling in love with her, but does nothing about it until Ruth, challenged by her mother-in-law, makes it known that

she is available. The only hitch is that she must be redeemed from an outstanding debt. Boaz can't marry her without first dealing with her personal liabilities. But that responsibility belonged to someone else. In Israel redemptive rights fell first to the closest kin. In other words, the redeemer needed to be related by blood. Boaz had the means to redeem Ruth and was willing but was second in line to do so. There was another man closer, who upon giving up his right allowed Boaz to redeem her. The Hebrew word *gaal* means "to redeem" and carries the idea of buying out the debt of a relative. Jesus is seen as our kinsman redeemer. As God, He has the means to pay the debt. As a human being, He is related to us by flesh. The parallels are not only striking in this manner but also carry with them other deep and beautiful truths. Boaz and Ruth, redeemer and redeemed, fall in love. This is extremely significant for those who feel that God's rescue process involves forcing us into a relationship with Him. The New Testament understanding of Christ's blood is that it is the purchase or redemption price necessary to rescue sinners from the "marketplace" of sin.

2. The words *ransom* and *atonement* are closely related. Traditionally the word *atonement*, from the Hebrew verb *kaphar*, has been translated "to cover." The idea is that the blood of animals only hid sin from God's eyes and did not deal with it in the manner of cleansing or washing away to make perfectly clean. It was the substitutionary blood of Jesus that would do more than just hide sin. It would take it away permanently. Old Testament sacrifices simply covered over sin until the Messiah came to deal with it once and for all. The *Theological Wordbook of the Old Testament, 1* says that the word *kaphar* is really derived from the noun *kopher* and means "to provide a ransom." (R. Laird Harris, Bruce K. Waltke, and Gleason L. Archer, Jr.. *Theological Wordbook of the Old Testament, 1* [Chicago: Moody Press, 1980], 453). In this case it would distinctly carry the idea of substitution, where someone else pays the price for another's offense.

3. To make propitiation (*hilaskomai*) means "to satisfy the demands of another." It is also translated "merciful" as in the case of Luke 18:13, "'God be merciful to me a sinner!'" The scriptural idea of propitiation must not be confused with the pagan notion of appeasement. The thought of a deity demanding satisfaction in a cruel and heartless manner is far from the New Testament truth where God is satisfied by the obedience of His Son. God is appeased by what Jesus did for us and not by what we can do for God on our own.

4. By definition *sin* is "missing the mark." But there has to be an established mark to shoot at before it can be missed. This is where the idea of a universal covenant, one every human being is responsible for, comes in. No such covenant is mentioned in Scripture, but it seems impossible

for anything other than for this to be true. If such a covenant does exist, it may be God's way of saying to humanity that in allowing us residency on His earth, we must abide by certain basic rules. In the Book of Romans God acknowledges a kind of intuitive knowledge of good and evil in every human being. "For the wrath of God is revealed from heaven against all ungodliness and unrighteousness of men, who suppress the truth in unrighteousness, because what may be known of God is manifest in them, for God has shown it to them. For since the creation of the world His invisible attributes are clearly seen, being understood by the things that are made, even His eternal power and Godhead, so that they are without excuse" (Rom. 1:18–20).

5.   Dwight Lyman Moody, *New Sermons, Addresses and Prayers* (Chicago: Henry S. Goodspeed, 1877), 158.

6.   Kenneth Wuest, *Hebrews in the Greek New Testament* (Grand Rapids, MI: Wm. B. Eerdmans Publishing Company, 1956), 159.

7.   For as much as sin's power and penalty are taken care of through the death and resurrection of Jesus, there are times when the scars of sin still remain—a bad marriage, a life of crime, or some kind of violent behavior produce undesirable effects—a wayward child, alimony payments, time spent in jail. Forgiveness seems to say that everything should be restored to its original condition. But that is not always the case. Broken marriages may eventually find forgiveness, but may not be restored. That is not to say that God is not concerned with bringing us to a place of restoration that brings happiness and joy.

CHAPTER 12: THE POWER OF SUBSTITUTION

1.   Trumbull, *The Blood Covenant*, 26.

2.   Ibid., 27–28.

CHAPTER 13: PASSOVER: COMMEMORATING THE OLD COVENANT

1.   The Jewish people trace their heritage more so to their exodus from Egypt than to Abraham. Harold Kushner says, "In a real sense, Passover is where Judaism begins. This is what turned the descendants of Abraham, Isaac, and Jacob into a people summoned by God, a people into whose collective life God suddenly erupted with His liberating message." (Kushner, *To Life!*, 124.)

     In the Passover Haggadah (the order of the Seder, that is, the community service that commemorates the exodus from Egypt), in the section called the "Four Kinds of Sons," the good son identifies himself with his ancestors as opposed to the wicked son who separates himself from his ancestors. The good son says, "This is what God did for *me* when He brought *me* out of Egypt" while the wicked son says, "This is what He did for *them* when He brought *them* out of Egypt."

To quote Martin Luther, "Therefore a man can with confidence boast in Christ and say: 'Mine are Christ's living, doing, and speaking, his suffering and dying, mine as much as if I had lived, done, spoken, suffered, and died as he did.'" (Timothy F. Lull and William R. Russell, eds., *Martin Luther's Basic Theological Writings* [Minneapolis, MN: Fortress Press, 2012]. Viewed online at Google Books.) This is the meaning of "in Christ," which is discussed at length in chapter 28.

CHAPTER 14: THE SIGNATURE OF THE NEW COVENANT

1. Ray C. Stedman, *Hebrews* (Downers Grove, IL: InterVarsity Press, 1992), 87.

CHAPTER 15: THE STIPULATIONS OF THE NEW COVENANT

1. In *Christian Theology* Millard J. Erickson says, "It is popularly held that whereas salvation in the New Testament era is obtained through faith, Old Testament saints were saved by fulfilling the law. Close examination of Old Testament texts belies this assumption, however. Actually, the important factor was the covenant God established with his people by grace; the law was simply the standard God set for those people who would adhere to that covenant. So it is said of Abraham that 'he believed God, and it was credited to him as righteousness.' Paul makes clear that Abraham's salvation was by faith, not by works of the law (Gal. 3:6). In numerous ways the Old Testament itself points out that it is not fulfillment of the law that saves a person. The law itself prescribed complete and unqualified love for God: 'love the LORD your God with all your heart, and with all your soul, and with all your strength' (Deut. 6:5). It similarly commanded love for one's neighbor: 'love your neighbor as yourself' (Lev. 19:18). If personal fulfillment of this law had been required of the Old Testament saints, none of them would have been saved. Clearly, salvation came through faith rather than works. Furthermore, although the covenant between God and man was certified by an external ritual, namely, circumcision, that act alone was insufficient to make a person right with God. There had to be a circumcision of the heart as well (Deut. 10:16; Jer. 4:4). That act of faith was the crucial factor." (Millard J. Erickson, *Christian Theology* [Grand Rapids, MI: Baker Book House, 1983, 1984, 1985, 1998], 988.)

2. Horatius Bonar, "Not Faith, But Christ," http://www.monergism.com/ththreshold/articles/onsite/everlasting.html (accessed November 12, 2013).

CHAPTER 16: WASHED IN BLOOD

1. G. Campbell Morgan, *The Bible and the Cross* (Grand Rapids, MI: Baker Book House, 1975).

2. Again notice Millard J. Erickson's statement from the notes of chapter 15: "Actually, the important factor was the covenant God established with his people by grace; the law was simply the standard God set for those people who would adhere to that covenant." We have it backward if we look to the Law or to our own righteousness to gain God's favor. We are already in His favor by grace. Once in He makes known the way things work for good by introducing the Law.

3. This story is widely circulated and used as a sermon illustration.

4. H. A. Maxwell Whyte, *The Power of the Blood* (Springfield, PA: Whitaker House, 1973), 27–28.

CHAPTER 17: A RADICAL SUBSTITUTION

1. Because, in this world, we are still capable of sinning, there are deep questions as to just how far the cleansing power of Christ's blood goes. We are certain that it cleanses former sin, but what about present and future sin? Does having an advocate (lawyer) mean that anything that happens is automatically taken care of, or does there have to be confession and repentance for the blood to go to work again? Is John's "If we confess our sins, He is faithful and just to forgive us our sins and to cleanse us from all unrighteousness" (1 John 1:9) a confession that takes place only at salvation, or is it is to be ongoing? If it is something that needs to happen every time we sin, why the words "cleanse us from all unrighteousness"? Certainly many Christians feel the need to confess whatever sin is at hand. It might be well to consider Romans 8:34, "Who *is* he who condemns? *It is* Christ who died, and furthermore is also risen, who is even at the right hand of God, who also makes intercession for us." Other related questions exist: If a Christian dies before he can ask forgiveness for a sin just committed, would he go to hell? What happens to Christians whose minds falter as they get older and consequently do sinful things? What happens to their sin? While most of what could be said might be little more than speculation, one thing is clear: God is a good God and never makes mistakes. His mercy endures forever! His plan in taking care of sin through Jesus is much greater than our current understanding. "For Christ also suffered once for sins, the just for the unjust, that He might bring us to God, being put to death in the flesh but made alive by the Spirit" (1 Pet. 3:18).

2. Leon Morris, *The Apostolic Preaching of the Cross* (Grand Rapids, MI: Wm. B. Eerdman Publishing Co., 1965), 61.

3. Wuest, *Hebrews in the Greek New Testament*, 159.

4. Charles F. Pfeiffer, *The Epistle to the Hebrews* (Chicago: The Moody Bible Institute, 1962). Viewed online at Google Books.

5. Historically there has been debate over the concept of "sin-bearing" in the form of substitution. The strongest biblical argument is that of "penal substitution" (from the Greek *poena* meaning punishment or penalty). The idea is that the substitute bears the penalty for sin by stepping in to take the place of punishment of another. By doing so the guilt of one is transferred to the other. Some, however, have erroneously argued against this position in favor of what is called "penitent substitution." The thought is that our sin is "absorbed" by Christ on the basis of His acknowledgment of God's hatred for it. Further, the suffering Christ is sufficient payment for our sins and a penitent heart is all that is necessary for God's forgiveness. Although we would never want to diminish the importance of the pain that Christ suffered, there is no evidence to support the idea that His pre-cross suffering cleansed a single sin. The Scriptures teach that it was in His death and the shedding of His blood by which we were saved from sin. John R. W. Stott says: "It is clear from Old Testament usage that to 'bear sin' means neither to sympathize with sinners, nor to identify with their pain, nor to express their penitence, nor to be persecuted on account of human sinfulness (as others have argued), nor even to suffer the consequences of sin in personal or social terms, but specifically to endure its penal consequences, to undergo its penalty." (John R. W. Stott, *The Cross of Christ* [Downers Grove, IL: InterVarsity Press, 1986, 2006], 143). A further note: Although only Christ's death can offer payment for sin, we can still say that it was through His life (and not that of another) that we obtain salvation (Rom. 5:10). These are not opposing truths.

CHAPTER 18: COMMUNION: CELEBRATING THE NEW COVENANT

1. Some churches take Communion weekly, pointing to Acts 20:7, while others receive it monthly, as 1 Corinthians 11:26 says "as often as you eat this bread and drink this cup," seems to indicate it can be taken less frequently. We must remember that when God wants something done specifically, He spells it out in detail. For this reason we must not look at Communion legalistically. What is most important is that when we partake of Communion, we do it "in remembrance of Him." There are, however, those who believe that Communion is a spiritual observance and should not be "taken" at all. This is unquestionably in violation of the Scriptures and clearly a mark of deception.

2. Transubstantiation is the belief that the bread and wine taken at Communion are literally transformed into the real body and blood of Jesus.

The eating and the drinking of Christ's body and blood that He spoke of in John 6:53 is a figurative statement concerning identification with Him. To make it literal confuses the ordinance and detracts from our understanding of blood covenant and the power of Jesus's blood. On the other hand, we must realize that Jesus is definitely present in Spirit at the table. This is a concept some call contra-substantiation.

CHAPTER 20: NOBODY CAN TOUCH THE BABY

1. Gordon Dunn, "The Martyrdom of John and Betty Stam," http://www.omf.org/omf/us/resources__1/omf_archives/china_inland_mission_stories/the_martyrdom_of_john_and_betty_stam (accessed November 13, 2013).

2. Many Christians and theologians believe that in the "last days" God is going to take His people out of the world (in an event called the Rapture) before the Tribulation, a period of time filled with great suffering, misery, and pain such as the world has never seen (Dan. 12:1–3).

CHAPTER 21: GOD'S PURPOSE IN COVENANT MAKING

1. The virgin birth allowed Jesus to access our world as a human being without the taint of sin. (See Note 2 in chapter 3.) It is quite clear from Scripture that the incarnation was not and could not have been of human initiative; otherwise it would have instilled the sin nature into the God nature of Jesus. God sent His Son, and He did so through a virgin. It is also clear that Mary was not without sin. The Bible clearly says every human being is "born in sin." Because of the virgin birth, her sin was not transferred to Jesus.

CHAPTER 23: ENTERING GOD'S PRESENCE

1. The measurements given are taken from the view that a cubit (the ancient measurement used for the tabernacle) was the distance from the tip of a man's hand to his elbow, or about eighteen inches. Thus, five cubits would be about seven and a half feet in length. However, archaeological evidence now suggests that a cubit was actually a little over twenty-one inches in length. "Cubit sticks" have been found in numerous digs, such as King Tut's tomb, and measure this new length.

2. Whyte, *The Power of the Blood*, 31.

CHAPTER 24: POWER IN THE BLOOD

1. R. A. Torrey, *How to Obtain Fullness of Power* (Tarrytown, NY: Fleming H. Revell Company, 1897; Murfreesboro, TN: Sword of the Lord Publishers, 2000), 19.

2. Whyte, *The Power of the Blood*, 74.

CHAPTER 28: THE WONDER OF BEING "IN CHRIST"

1. A. W. Tozer, *Christ the Eternal Son*, compiled and edited by Gerald B. Smith (Harrisburg, PA: Christian Publications, Inc., 1982), 17.

2. Romans 7:1–4 uses the analogy of a woman married to a husband to illustrate the idea of being bound in sin. The law binds her to her husband so long as he lives. Only if he dies is she free from him. What kept us bound to and in sin was the Law. It kept us married to sin, by always reminding us of our sin (Rom. 3:20). But we were made dead to the Law through the body of Christ. He died for our sin, leaving the Law with nothing to which we might be bound, and thus making us free to then be joined to Christ. By virtue of being joined to Him we now bear fruit unto God rather than bearing fruit unto death as a result of being in the flesh.

3. Alex Altman, "Chesley B. Sullenberger III," January 16, 2009, http://content.time.com/time/nation/article/0,8599,1872247,00.html (accessed November 14, 2013).

4. "My Trust," author unknown, in *742 Heart-Warming Poems*, comp. by John R. Rice (n.p.: Sword of the Lord Publishers, 1982). Viewed online at Google Books.

5. There is much disagreement about whose faith saves us. The contention is whether we are saved by "our own" faith "in" Jesus or by the faith that is "of and in" Him apart from anything we could remotely say is in us. At issue is the different uses of the Greek in translating the phrase in Galatians 2:16 as "in Christ Jesus." The contention is that the best translation of this part of the verse should be "of Christ Jesus" and not "in," which would mean it is His faith and not ours that saves us. In considering this argument, a good point to remember is that even if I do have some type of "initial faith," I cannot brag, be confident in myself, or even rest in my own faith, whatever that looks like. It is faith developed in me by His Word and by His Spirit. So then it is true that much of our faith did, in fact, reside first in Him and we did get it by His influence, but God also speaks of a faith that we have within ourselves.

6. Dictionary.com, s.v. "grace," http://dictionary.reference.com/browse/grace (accessed November 14, 2013).

7. Ibid.

8. In personal communication with the author. Used with permission.

Other Books by Ray Beeson

- *The Real Battle*
- *That I Might Know Him*
- *Spiritual Warfare and Your Children* (cowritten with Kathi Mills)
- *Strategic Spiritual Warfare* (cowritten with Patricia Hulsey)
- *The Hidden Price of Greatness* (cowritten with Ranelda Mack Hunsicker)
- *Create in Me a Clean Heart*
- *In Memory of Joseph Greycloud*
- *Don't Miss the Point*
- *The Spirit-Filled Life Bible for Students*

If you are interested in ordering more copies of this book or copies of the books above, please go to your local bookstore or contact Overcomers Ministries at www.overcomersministries .net.

EMPOWERED
TO RADICALLY CHANGE
YOUR WORLD

Charisma House brings you books, e-books, and other media from dynamic Spirit-filled Christians who are passionate about God.

Check out all of our releases from best-selling authors like **Jentezen Franklin**, **Perry Stone**, and **Kimberly Daniels** and experience God's supernatural power at work.

**CHARISMA
HOUSE**

www.charismahouse.com

twitter.com/charismahouse • facebook.com/charismahouse